A Rwandan Bishop's Confession

A Rwandan Bishop's Confession

Mother Tongue Use and Primal Religion in
the Writings of Bishop Aloys Bigirumwami

Joel Kubwimana

FOREWORD BY
Gillian Mary Bediako

RESOURCE *Publications* • Eugene, Oregon

A RWANDAN BISHOP'S CONFESSION
Mother Tongue Use and Primal Religion in the Writings
of Bishop Aloys Bigirumwami

Resource Publications
An Imprint of Wipf and Stock Publishers
199 W. 8th Ave., Suite 3
Eugene, OR 97401

www.wipfandstock.com

PAPERBACK ISBN: 978-1-6667-0316-0
HARDCOVER ISBN: 978-1-6667-0317-7
EBOOK ISBN: 978-1-6667-0318-4

08/09/21

The book is dedicated to the memory of Bishop Aloys Bigirumwami (1904–1986), for his commitment to the incarnation of the Christian faith in Africa and particularly in Rwanda.

Contents

Foreword

IN THIS GROUND-BREAKING WORK, Joel Kubwimana explores an aspect of Rwandan Catholic Christian history from an entirely new perspective, namely, how the earliest African Catholic bishop of Rwanda, Aloys Bigirumwami, made the spiritual and intellectual journey from the radical break with his cultural setting necessitated by a strict missionary upbringing and education to the rediscovery of the importance of the mother tongue, Kinyarwanda, and the pre-Christian religious traditions and culture for the task of mission and evangelism and the rooting the Christian gospel deeply in Rwandan culture. He gives a well-researched account of Bigirumwami's efforts in this direction in his life's journey of research, teaching, pastoral ministry, and writing.

Drawing on Bigirumwami's published writings, in French and Kinyarwanda, as well as some hitherto unpublished material, Kubwimana builds a cogent argument. His facility in French and Kinyarwanda, as well as English, enables him to provide translations from both languages. The outcome is a fascinating insight into Rwandan Catholic Christian and missionary history and one pioneer bishop's intellectual and spiritual journey. It is possible that Kubwimana is also the first non-Catholic to investigate Rwandan Catholic Christian history as being of relevance to the church in Rwanda as a whole.

Kubwimana comes to the sobering conclusion that Bigirumwami was a prophet ahead of his time, who foresaw the potential for genocide before it took place in 1994, on the grounds that the Christian faith was not sufficiently deeply rooted in Rwandan society. Bigirumwami saw as the remedy for this a recovery of tradition and the rooting of Christian faith in local idiom.

If Bigirumwami was right, then the church in Africa still has much work to do in recovering the traditions of the past, so that they may be engaged with the gospel message, and in restoring Africa's heart languages to their rightful place at forefront of church life, Christian scholarship, and ministry. In view of the pervading onslaught of the so-called world languages in our time, this timely book points church leaders, theologians, pastors, lay leaders, and all thoughtful Christians in the right direction.

Gillian Mary Bediako, PhD

Deputy Rector, Akrofi-Christaller Institute of Theology,
Mission and Culture, Akropong-Akuapem, Ghana
February 18, 2021

Acknowledgments

RWANDANS SAY THAT "UMUTWE umwe wifasha gusara," literarily "one head helps itself in madness," meaning "you cannot achieve a good result alone." Publishing this book was not my work alone; different people contributed and I would like to acknowledge them. I thank God for granting me health and strength to write this book.

I acknowledge my mentor, Prof. Gillian Mary Bediako. she supervised my work while I was doing my MTh, and recommended it to Wipf and Stock for publication. Her advice and corrections contributed to successful publication of this book.

I am also grateful to: my wife, Mutamuriza Grace, my children, Kubwimana Pleasure and Kubwimana Jolly Cathrine, for their love, encouragement, patience, prayers, smiles, songs, and stories while I was working on this publication. I would like to acknowledge my parents, Rev. Dr. Ndyamiyemenshi Nathan and Nyiramategeko Souzan, for their support. I would like to appreciate Bishop Niyonzima Samvura Jean Damascene and his family, Rev. Ndolimana Emmanuel and his family, Dr. Colin Macpherson, and Langham Literature; I'm grateful for your moral and financial support. I am also grateful to Kuradusenge Valens Boanerge and Uwimana Jean Damascene for their technical support.

Finally, I would like to acknowledge you who are going to read this book. My pray is that you will gain more new insights from it to help you play your part in the fulfillment of the Great Commission.

You are loved by God and his people.

Joel Kubwimana

Abbreviations

ACI	Akrofi-Christaller Institute
ADEPR	Association des Eglises de Pentecôte au Rwanda
AGI	Action Catholique des Foyers
CEPR	Conférence Episcopale du Rwanda
CMS	Church Missionary Society
DR-Congo	Democratic Republic of Congo
ed.	editor
eds.	editors
IT	information technology
JACT	Journal of African Christian Thought
Mgr.	Monseigneur
MLS	Mission Libre Suédoise
no.	number
NP	no place of publication mentioned
NPH	no house of publication mentioned
OT	Old Testament
PIASS	Protestant Institute of Arts and Social Sciences
PhD	Doctor of Philosophy
REA	Réveil Est–Africain
RIET	Rwandan Institute of Evangelical Theology

SBMPC	Société Belge de Missions Protestantes au Congo
UR	University of Rwanda
vol.	volume
WCC	World Council of Churches

Introduction

Semantic Use

IN TALKING ABOUT THE traditional beliefs in Rwandan society before the arrival of Western missionaries, I will use "primal religions" instead of the familiar term used by many Rwandan writers, "traditional religions." Why the use of "primal" and not "traditional"? Discussing terms used to describe African beliefs, Byang Kato points out that there is a battle of words concerning "African Traditional Religions."[1] He discussed many different words that have been used to describe African primal religions, such as: "animism," "idolatry," "paganism" and "heathenism," "fetishism," "witchcraft," "juju," "primitive religions," and "African traditional religions."[2] For Kato, "African traditional religions" is the most comprehensive title for the religions of Africa.[3] According to him, "[t]he religions are distinctively African, though similarities are traceable in the Caribbean Islands and other Latin American countries. The religions are traditional opposed to the new religions on the continent such as Islam and Christianity."[4] Though for Kato "African traditional religion" is the right title to use for African religions, other scholars have argued the opposite. An exploratory consultation

1. Kato, *Theological Pitfalls in Africa*, 18–24.
2. Kato, *Theological Pitfalls in Africa*, 18–24.
3. Kato, *Theological Pitfalls in Africa*, 24.
4. Kato, *Theological Pitfalls in Africa*, 24.

on "Primal World-Views, Christian Involvement in Dialogue with Traditional Thought Forms" was held at the Intsitute of Church and Society in Ibadan, Nigeria, in September 1973, under the auspices of the World Council of Churches (subunit on Dialogue with People of Living Faith and Ideologies), the All-African Conference of Churches, and the Theological Education Fund. The participants in the Ibadan conference chose to use the word "primal" instead of "traditional." According to them, "'primal' is used in the sense of 'basic' or 'fundamental,' and to refers to those forms of society or religion, or those forms of comprehensive reference-systems, which are associated with what are commonly called tribal peoples or cultures."[5] By considering primal as basic or fundamental, they point out that "it is not meant to suggest that these are more fundamental, authentic or 'true' than other religious systems, but simply that in historical fact they have been widely distributed across all continents and have preceded and contributed to all other known religious systems of mankind."[6] Apart from defining the word "primal," they further indicate the reason for choosing the word: "This term is chosen for working purposes to embrace what has been referred to in the past by a whole series of other terms, each of which is unacceptable today: e.g. pre-literate, primitive, pagan, animistic, primordial, native, ethnic, tribal and traditional."[7] The participants were aware of the fact that the term that was mostly in use at the time was "traditional." The reason why they stopped using the term "traditional" is that:

> "[T]raditional," is often used of indigenous African forms, it applies to all known religions, and especially to both Islam and Christianity, and is not distinctive of the religions of African origin to which it is being applied, nor of their counterparts in other continents. "Primal" is therefore intended to avoid objectionable or inaccurate alternatives, or judgmental words (whether derogatory or laudatory), and to suggest both the possession of basic

5. Taylor, *Primal World-Views*, 3.
6. Taylor, *Primal World-Views*, 3.
7. Taylor, *Primal World-Views*, 3–4.

religious forms and a factual historical relation to other religious systems.[8]

In concluding the definition of the term "primal," participants indicated, "while we may not yet have discovered an ideal term and while there must be a continuing search for improved terminology, this word seems less objectionable than others, is coming into more common usage, and is capable of assuming the meanings for which we require a comprehensive term."[9] The WCC Ibadan conference was not the only forum that preferred the use of "primal" in place of "traditional"; there are many others scholars who used and still use the term "primal" in reference to African pre-Christianity religions. According to Gillian M. Bediako:

> Primal is a positive term that denotes anteriority. Primal religions are prior to all religious traditions and underlie them all. Primal also means basal or elemental, the fundamental substratum to all subsequent religious experience, continuing to varying degrees in all later religious traditions.[10]

The word "primal" might be considered as another way of saying that primal religions are primitive religions or ancient religions, but according to the definition given by Gillian M. Bediako, it is clear that "primal" is taken as base, foundation. Thus, primal religions are not primitive religions, but the essential base of religions. Gillian Bediako's definition points out another important element to consider, that is, "continuity." Primal religions as substructure continue in different degrees to exist in major religions. Therefore, the use of "traditional religions" may not be appropriate because "traditional" may be replaced by "modern." Primal beliefs are observed and noticed in Christianity, Islam, Buddhism, and other dominant religions in the world. Therefore, the term "traditional" will not be used, but I shall not change where the word is used by quoted authors.

8. Taylor, *Primal World-Views*, 4.
9. Taylor, *Primal World-Views*, 4.
10. Bediako, "Primal Religion and Christian Faith," 12.

Bigirumwami's books, letters, and articles are my main source of study. It is good to indicate that in his time Kinyarwanda orthography was still at the stage of development or beginning. Therefore, those who know Kinyarwanda will notice a huge difference in the orthography of his time and what is used currently. It is the same case with his use of French. He preferred the archaic form of some words, such as "payenne" instead of "paienne."

Background and Motivation of Writing This Book

This book is based on a dissertation presented to the Akrofi-Christaller Institute of Theology, Mission and Culture in partial fulfillment for the award of Master of Theology in African Christianity. The topic of the dissertation was "Kinyarwanda as a Vehicle of the Primal: An Examination of the Life and Work of Bishop Aloys Bigirumwami with Particular Reference to His Advocacy of Mother-Tongue Use and His Perception of Rwandan Primal Religion." I arrived at Akrofi Christaller Institute with the understanding that all religions that existed in Africa before the spread of Christianity were "traditional religions." They were traditional in sense that they were superseded by world religions like Christianity, Islam, and Buddhism. Through the "Christian Faith and Primal Religions of the World, with Special Reference to Africa" (course), I came to the understanding that those religions cannot be substituted or eliminated, as they are the base, "the fundamental substratum to all subsequent religious experience, continuing to varying degree in all later religious traditions."[11] Seeing the need to deepen my knowledge and understanding of the primal religions, I started to think about different topics in the area. When I was working on the essay for the course, I came across Bigirumwami's confession before his death quoted by Paul Rutayisire,.[12] The quote that I'm using is from Bigirumwami himself:

11. Bediako, "Primal Religion and Christian Faith," 12.

12 Rutayisire, «Catholicisme Rwandais,» 259.

AMABUYE ABIRI IYO AKORANYE AVAMO URU-
MURI: De deux chos [*sic*] jaillit lumière! Kuli iki
gihe, mu Rwanda hali amadini abili: UBUPAGANI
n'UBUKRISTU. Mbabajwe nuko ntabimenye kera
kose, ngihabwa Ubusaserdoti mu wa 1929. Mbabajwe
n'uko muli iyo myaka nigishije ubukristu mbwangisha
ubupagani, nsha ubupagani mu Rwanda, ntazi icyo
mbuziza ! Mbabajwe n'uko Ubukristu butarashinga
imizi mu Rwanda n'igihe bumaze ! Mbabajwe n'uko jye
nabandi, ubukristu twabuhagitse mu giti cy'ubupagani,
nk'abahagika umuzinga mu giti ! Murumva ko igiti
n'umuzinga bitagira ihuliro.[13]

[When two stones collide against each other, it gives
light! From two things erupt light! Currently, in Rwanda
we have two religions: "PAGANISM" and CHRISTIAN-
ITY. I regret not to have known this since 1929 when
I was ordained into the priesthood. During those years,
I regret having taught Christianity by opposing it to
"paganism," wanting to eradicate paganism in Rwanda,
without knowing the reason for its eradication. I regret
to notice that Christianity is not rooted in Rwanda, despite many years of presence. I regret having with others,
suspended Christianity in the branches of paganism, just
as a hive is suspended in the branches of a tree. It is clear
that under these conditions, the tree and the hive cannot
communicate, they are entirely opposed.][14]

Two reasons therefore motivated the choice of my dissertation
which resulted into this publication: first, traditional religions and
primal religions; second, Bigirumwami's confession.

---

13. Bigirumwami, *Umuntu*, 99.

14. Most of the works of Bigirumwami used in this book were written
in Kinyarwanda, and a few in French. Besides Bigirumwami's works, I used
other works that are in Kinyarwanda or French. Throughout the book I translated some quotations either from Kinyarwanda to English or from French to
English. I used the square brackets [] to indicate my translations. Where the
translation is not mine, I indicate it by giving the source of the translation.

Bishop Aloys Bigirumwami was born on December 22, 1904[15] at Zaza in Rwanda. He was ordained as a Roman Catholic priest in 1926.[16] Apart from serving as priest, Bigirumwami wrote many books on Rwandan culture in Kinyarwanda. In doing this, he paid a great deal of attention to Rwandan primal religion. According to Léonidas Ngarukiyintwari (a priest from Nyundo), "Bigirumwami was a Christian who respected and gave value to the culture of our ancestors and this did not stop him from being a true Christian."[17] Normally, for a Christian to respect and value the culture of his/ her ancestors is not something special or uncommon. Therefore, it is very important to understand why Ngarukiyintwari emphasized the fact that giving value to the culture of our Rwandan ances- tors did not stop Bigirumwami from being a true Christian. The arrival of Western missionaries in Rwanda led to many political, economic, and sociocultural changes. There was incomprehen- sion among the European missionaries encountering Rwandan primal religions. Paul Rutayisire indicates that "the relationship of Catholic missionaries with Rwandan culture in general, and with traditional religions in particular has been predominantly one of conflict."[18] The conflict was based on the fact that for Western missionaries everything related to Rwandan culture was seen as evil, "pagan." When Bigirumwami started writing on Rwandan culture in positive way, he was considered to be unusual by some Rwandans, Ngarukiyimvura included. This same reason motivated me to study Bigirumwami's works focusing on his advocacy for mother tongue use and examination of his perception of Rwandan primal religion. This book is also a response to the call of Bigi- rumwami, who asked priests and pastors in Rwanda to carefully study Rwandans and their culture in order to reach them well with the gospel of Jesus Christ.[19] Knowing that in Rwanda we have few

15 Bushayija, *Musenyeri Aloys Bigirumwami*, 11.

16. Bigirumwami, *Umuntu*, 7.

17 Ngarukiyintwari, "Tumenye Umurage Twasigiwe n'umukurambere wacu."

18. Rutayisire, «Catholicisme Rwandais,» 258.

19. Bigirumwami, "A mes Frères dans le Sacerdoce."

written resources by Rwandans in theology, especially in the area of gospel and culture, which is dominated by Roman Catholic scholars, I decided to publish my dissertation.

The Problem Addressed by This Book

The fundamental problem addressed is that it was through the process of Christianizing Rwanda that Rwandan culture was demonized and Rwandan Christians were asked to abandon it. Two streams can be identified in contributing to this problem: Eurocentrism and Western missionaries' incomprehension of Rwandan culture.

The Catholic missionaries were the first to arrive in Rwanda in 1900[20] and started the work of spreading Christianity in Rwanda. Lutheran pastors Ernst Johanssen and Gerhard Ruccius, with some Tanzanian evangelists, were the first Protestant missionaries to arrive in Rwanda in 1907.[21] According to Rutinduka, between 1900 and 1917 the evangelization was not successful[22] and King Musinga was considered as the reason.[23] King Yuhi V Musinga was replaced by his son Mutara III Rudahigwa in 1931 and in 1946 King Rudahigwa took the momentous decision to consecrate Rwanda to the King of kings, Jesus Christ. From 1931, many

---

20. Rutinduka, «L'Église catholique au Rwanda,» 15.

21 Gatwa, «L'Église Presbytérienne au Rwanda,» 63–75.

22. Rutinduka, «L'Église catholique au Rwanda,» 17.

23. King Yuhi V. Musinga's resistance to convert to Christianity was the major obstacle for the Roman Catholic missionaries. Being in competition with Protestant missionaries who were then arriving, the Roman Catholic missionaries took advantage of the First World War defeat of the Germans, who had to leave their colonies. With the support of the new colonizers the Belgians, the Roman Catholic missionaries took the opportunity to lead in the deposition of Yuhi V Musinga in November 1931. According to Bishop Léon Paul Classe, King Yuhi V Musinga prevented his people from receiving baptism for the salvation of their soulss. Rutinduka, "L'Église catholique au Rwanda," 22.

Rwandans joined the church.[24] According to Rutinduka, two main reasons may explain the event.

First, there was the creation of the "Bayozefite" Josephites Brothers Congregation, made of Rwandese. The Bayozefite congregation was made of Rwandans who had the mission of helping Roman Catholic priests in the ministry of teaching the catechism, teaching religion in secondary schools, or carrying on other evangelistic activities. They played a remarkable role in spreading Christianity as local missionaries who could interact with their fellow Rwandans easily.

Second, *Irivuze umwami*,[25] meaning "the effect of what the king says." The East African Revival of 1930s also played a role in the spread of Christianity in Rwanda and the East African region. André Corten indicates that "the REA[26] emphasizes conversion rather than instruction; it takes up hymns of African origin and gives them a significant place."[27] The use of mother tongue songs made it possible for the East African Revival to play a role in the process of spreading Christianity in Rwanda. Rwanda thus became a Christian kingdom where everyone had to turn from paganism and become a new creature in Christ. How Rwanda reached the level of being known as a Christian nation is examined in the second chapter. The main method used by both Catholic and Protestant missionaries in evangelization was to make Rwandans deny their culture in order to accept the gospel. Everything related to Rwandan culture was seen as evil or pagan; therefore, a Christian had to completely and publicly declare that he/she renounced all traditions and customs before being baptized. Rutayisere writes that "The converts had to renounce their cultural identity and show zeal in the hunt for the signs of paganism."[28]

After reading Bigirumwami's confession, I asked myself some questions: (1) Why did a Christian leader like Bigirumwami regret

24. Rutinduka, «L'Église catholique au Rwanda,» 22.

25. Rutinduka, «L'Église catholique au Rwanda,» 22.

26. Réveil est-africain.

27. Corten, «Rwanda,» 28.

28. Rutayisire, «Le Catholisme Rwandais, «258.

propagating Christianity at the expense of primal religion? (2) How did he come to the realization that being opposed to primal religion out of devotion to Christianity was in itself not good for the Christian faith?

To address the above questions, I explored the impact of the Western missionaries' negative views of Rwandan culture on the first Rwandans converted to Christianity. This is well developed in the second chapter, where I discuss the spread of Christianity in Rwanda and its impact. In the third and fourth chapters, I indicate how the Kinyarwanda language was the vehicle by which Bigirumwami came to the realization that Rwandan primal religion is not entirely bad and in fact it is important for an appreciation of the Christian faith.

Uniqueness of the Book

The studied thesis cuts across several fields of study. These fields include the general field of Christian historical studies, under which African Christianity falls, specifically researching the area of mother tongue use and the practice of primal religion in Rwanda. Building on the earlier work of Andrew Walls[29] and Harold Turner[30] on primal religion, Kwame Bediako in his scholarly works emphasized the importance of the mother tongue and primal religion in the spread of Christianity in Africa.

> The ability to hear in one's own language and to express in one's own language one's response to the message which one receives, must lie at the heart of all authentic religious encounter with the divine realm. Language itself becomes, then, not merely a social or a psychological phenomenon, but a theological one as well. Though every language has its limitations in this connection, yet it is through language, and for each person, through their mother tongue, that the Spirit of God speaks to

---

29. Walls, "Gospel as the Prisoner and Liberator," 93–105.

30. Turner, "Primal Religions."

convey divine communication at its deepest to the human community.[31]

For Kwame Bediako, the mother tongue is crucial in religious encounter and language is not to be seen as just a means of communication but also as theology. Despite its limitations, language is still the vehicle that conveys the divine message to humans. The mother tongue has not only the ability to convey the divine message; it is also the vehicle that conveys the primal imagination of people. Discussing theological creativity in the mother tongue, Philip T. Laryea indicates that "European languages cannot convey the truths about African spirituality, since language does not entail only grammar, but is, in fact, the vehicle that carries the culture and the entire world view of people."[32] Laryea points out an important role of language. Language is a vehicle, a channel that helps us to understand or to know the culture and the worldview of particular people. You cannot understand the Rwandan worldview through French or English, but through Kinyarwanda. On the other hand, the mother tongue may help people to retain their worldview. Discussing the persistence of a traditional worldview in the spiritual churches[33] in Africa, Bediako indicates that:

> [T]he persistence of the traditional world-view lies in the spiritual churches' vernacular hearing and perception of the Christian evangel through the vernacular Scriptures. The combination of this vernacular reading of the Bible with the earnest desire to arrive at African answers and solutions to *African* questions and problems, has the effect of making the living forces of the traditional world-view persist longer and with greater potency within the 'spiritual churches' than in the churches of missionary origin.[34]

31. Bediako, *Christianity in Africa*, 60.

32. Laryea, "Letting the Gospel Re-Shape Culture," 31.

33. African independent churches are also called "spiritual churches." Bediako, *Christianity in Africa*, 63.

34. Bediako, *Christianity in Africa*, 66.

In this case, the vernacular Scriptures serve as bridge,[35] vehicle, or channel[36] that links people to their primal worldview. On the other hand, the vernacular Scriptures make "the living forces of the traditional world view persist longer."[37] The vernacular or mother tongue plays a double role: it helps in understanding and interpreting the Scriptures well, but on the other hand it may help to root people to their primal worldview.

It is with the understanding of the mother tongue as the vehicle to the primal understanding of people, as indicated by Bediako and Laryea, that I have examined the works of Aloys Bigirumwami.

Steps Involved in Understanding Bigirumwami's Thought

Three types of literature were used: documents written by Bigirumwami, documents written about Bigirumwami, and documents that helped me to place Bigirumwami in the intellectual framework and the context of his time. Conversations with Bernardin Muzungu, Antoni B. Bugabo, and Gapfizi Felicien were of great help in getting to the sources and filling in the gaps of available written documents.

Literature Written by Bigirumwami

Bernardin Muzungu, a Roman Catholic priest and famous Rwandan theologian and historian who lived and worked with Bigirumwami, in his article "Bishop Aloys Bigirumwami, a Shining Star in the Political Darkness of Rwanda," gave a list of Bigirumwami's great publications in a chronological order: "*Imigani migufu* (Proverbs) in 1967; *Imigani miremire* (moral Tales), in 1971; *Ibitekerezo* (Oral tradition) in 1971; *Imihango* (Habits rituals), in 1974; *Imana y'Abantu–Imana mu Bantu* (Religious anthropology), in 1976;

---

35. Bediako, *Christianity in Africa*, 66.

36. Laryea, "Letting the Gospel Re-Shape Culture," 31.

37. Bediako, *Christianity in Africa*, 66.

Umuntu (Christian Anthropology), in 1983."[38] From the given list, only two books were analyzed. The two books were chosen based on the fact that they are not collections like the other listed books, but are Bigirumwami's perceptions of Rwandans, their culture, and Christianity. The first book studied is *Imana y'Abantu—Imana mu Bantu*, literally meaning "God of people—God among people," real meaning "The Creator and Redeemer." In this book, Bigirumwami discusses creation[39] and redemption.[40] The book was useful in examining the views of Bigirumwami concerning Rwandan primal religion. In this book, Bigirumwami discusses natural revelation and special revelation, indicating that through natural revelation all humans know the existence of God, and good and evil, and have the knowledge of life after death. Concerning special revelation, he indicates how through the incarnation of Jesus Christ those who believed in him (Christians) were able to go beyond the knowledge of the existence of God and reach the level of knowing that God dwells among them. For Bigirumwami, special revelation is the reason why Christians must carry on the mission of spreading the gospel. For Bigirumwami, it is important to know that people have images of Christ in their traditions. Therefore, it is good to use those images as a point of contact in reaching out to people with the gospel of Jesus Christ. The book also points out that the culture or traditions of people cannot be entirely evil; there are two sides: a good side and an evil side. Thus, the gospel is capable of pointing out to people what is good from their traditions and what it is evil that the gospel can convert.

The second book examined is *Umuntu: Baribwira, Barabwirwa, Batereriyo*, literally meaning "Humans: They Talk to Themselves, They Are Told, and They Don't Care." The book is talking about three types of humans.[41] It is presented like an encyclopedia in which the author is trying to present a summary of his previous

38 Muzungu, "Bishop ALoys Bigirumwami," 71.

39. Bigirumwami, *Imana y'Abantu*, 5–11.

40. Bigirumwami, *Imana y'Abantu*, 27–29.

41. Bigirumwami, *Umuntu*, 7–10.

books.[42] Due to the fact that I was aware that some articles written by Bigirumwami relating to Rwandan primal religion are not available either due to their destruction during the genocide perpetrated against the Tutsi in 1994, or because they are located in Roman Catholic archives in Rwanda, Rome, and Belgium and time and financial constraints rendered them inaccessible for this research, this book was helpful in filling in some of the information complementing the first book mentioned above. The book also deals with Rwandan primal religion, the spread of Christianity in Rwanda, and the first white fathers' attitudes towards Rwandan traditions and concept of Imana (God).

Knowing that some Western Roman Catholic missionaries would like to know what he was writing in Kinyarwanda, Bigirumwami used to write an introductory letter and at the end of each chapter, a summary in French. An introductory letter in the book *Imihango idakwiye* and summaries of chapters were examined. The letter to his brothers in priesthood presented in the book *IMIHANGO: n'Imigenzo, n'Imiziririzo mu Rwanda* and the article "Usages, Tabous et Practiques Traditionnels Dans la Vie Coutummière Au Rwanda" (meaning "Usages, Taboos and Traditional Practices of Daily Life in Rwanda") annexed in the book were studied. The letters and summaries are not corrections but Bigirumwami's presentation to non-Kinyarwanda readers. This makes them important, as they indicate how Bigirumwami was concerned by Western missionaries' negative view of Rwandan culture.

In 1969, a refresher seminar for priests and scholars took place at Nyundo on "Culture traditionnelle et Christianisme" ["Traditional Culture and Christianity"]. The seminar was organized by the Nyundo diocese at the time administered by Bishop Aloys Bigirumwami. Apart from being the one who opened the seminar officially, Bigirumwami also presented a paper on "Rites, Proverbes, et Fables au Rwanda"[43] ["Rites, Proverbs, and Fables

---

42. Editions du Secrétariat général de la CEPR, *Homage a Mgr Aloys Bigirumwami première Evêque rwandais*, 97.

43. Nyundo Diocese, *Recyclage Sacerdotal sur Culture Traditionnelle et Christianisme*, 3–13.

in Rwanda"]. The views that Bigirumwami presented in this paper and the reaction of the participants at the end of the paper were examined. Being the first seminar focusing on Christianity and primal religion organized in Rwanda, the outcomes of the conference played a role in calling up other priests and lay Roman Catholics to give much attention to mother tongue use and appreciation of the value and role of Rwandan traditions in the inculturation of the Christian faith in Rwanda. Through this conference the Roman Catholic Bible translators were asked to give much importance to mother tongue for a successful translation, as the first missionaries used mixed languages of Luganda, Swahili, and Kinyarwanda, which did not allow the gospel to penetrate the hearts of Rwandans.

Literature about Bigirumwami

The few books and articles that have been written on Bigirumwami are mostly by Rwandan Roman Catholic priests and members. Antoni Bugabo Bushayija, a professor of history, wrote a biography with the title *Musenyeri Aloys Bigirumwami,* meaning "Bishop Aloys Bigirumwami." Bushayija, who visited the white fathers archives of Rome and the archives of Tervuren–Bruxelles–Belgique, did a great job in terms of writing about the life of Bigirumwami. Therefore, I did not focus much on the life of Bigirumwami. However, Bushayija does not examine the books and articles of Bigirumwami. Bushayija's book was helpful as it contains some important letters in the annexes, such as the letter of Bigirumwami's father, speeches on the day of Bigirumwami's consecration as bishop, and praise, songs, and poems for Bigirumwami. The letter of Rukamba that Bushayija presented was useful in knowing the role of his father in consecrating him to God so that he could serve God as priest.

The publishing arm of the General Secretariat of Conférence Episcopale du Rwanda (CEPR) published a book containing testimonies presented on the day of commemorating fifty years (1959–2009) of the ecclesiastical hierarchy institution in Rwanda.

The testimonies focussed on Bigirumwami as the first Rwandan bishop. The book points out the contributions of Bigirumwami to the church and Rwandan society, as well as providing a long list of books, articles, and letters of Bigirumwami and summarizing what Bigirumwami said.[44] The book does not critically examine particular works of Bigirumwami, but it was helpful in discussing the ministry of Bigirumwami as a priest, the creation of Nyundo vicariate, and the legacy of Bigirumwami.

In his journal *Les Cahiers Lumière et Société*, Bernadin Muzungu wrote an article in Kinyarwanda, French, and English on Bigirumwami, titled "Bishop Aloys Bigirumwami: A Shining Star in the Political Darkness of Rwanda."[45] Muzungu focuses on the political role of Bigirumwami in Rwanda. The article was helpful in directing me to other sources and I had an opportunity to meet the author of the article and ask him about how to get those sources, especially the ones on his website.

Contextual Studies

I used different publications in locating Birumwami in an intellectual framework. The works of the following authors were used in putting Bigirumwami in a broader context, especially Andrew Walls[46] and Harold Turner[47] for the world context and the following for the African context: Kwame Bediako, *Christianity in Africa: The Renewal of a Non-Western Religion*[48]; Philip T. Laryea, *"Letting the Gospel Re-Shape Culture: Theological Creativity In Mother Tongue"*[49]; Gillian M. Bediako, *"Primal Religion and Christian Faith: Antagonist or Souls-Mates?"*[50]; and Andrew Walls, *The*

44. Editions du Secrétariat général de la CEPR, *Homage a Mgr Aloys Bigirumwami*, 75–94.

45. Muzungu, "Bishop Aloys Bigirumwami," 61–86.

46. Walls, "Gospel as the Prisoner and Liberator," 93–105.

47. Turner, "Primal Religions."

48. Bediako, *Christianity in Africa*.

49. Laryea, "Letting the Gospel Re-Shape Culture."

50. Bediako, "Primal Religion and Christian Faith."

Missionary Movement in Christian History: Studies in the Transmission of Faith.[51] Concerning situating Bigirumwami in his context, books on the history of Rwanda and the history of Christianity in Rwanda were used. The book *Un Royaume Hamite au Centre de l'Afrique* (meaning "A Hamitic Kingdom in the Center of Africa") by Pagès is the earliest historical book written on Rwanda. The book introduces the ethnic groups and stereotypes in Rwanda. The book was helpful in examining how Bigirumwami dealt with the issues of ethnicity and origin of people, especially Rwandans. *Inganji Kalinga*[52] (meaning "Kalinga Reign") by Alexis Kagame[53] was the first historical book on Rwanda written by a Rwandan. The book was written in Kinyarwanda as the author wanted the majority of Rwandans to be able to read it.[54] Kagame clearly indicates that the first books on Rwanda were written by Western scholars, giving them a Western orientation.[55] For him, they did not portray the true image of Rwanda and the history of Rwanda was distorted. In his writing, he clearly indicates that he sought information from Rwandans, especially elders, making his book a reflection of oral tradition.[56] Alexis Kagame was not, however, able to avoid the Western approach in terms of the origin of Rwandans. Semujanga indicates that Kagame maintained the Hamitic myth advanced by Louis de Lacger, but situated it in Africa due to his African nationalistic ideology.[57] To clarify the controversy, I used other books such as L'Histoire du Rwanda Precolonial (meaning "Precolonial History of Rwanda") by Muzungu Bernard and *Les Défis de l'Historiographie Rwandaise: Les Faits Controversée*

51. Walls, *Missionary Movement in Christian History.*

52. Kalinga was a royal drum symbolizing the power of the Nyiginya kingdom.

53. Alexis Kagame (1912–1981), Rwandan poet, historian, ethologist, linguist, and Roman Catholic priest, wrote and published many books and articles on Rwanda and Bantu philosophy.

54. Alexis Kagame, *Inganji Kalinga*, 15.

55. Kagame, *Inganji Kalinga*, 15–17.

56. Kagame, *Inganji Kalinga*, 17–19.

57. Semujanga, «Discours scientifique,» 41–42.

("The Challenges of Rwandan Historiography: The Controversial Issues"). The second book was written under the direction of Byanafashe Déogratias, who was the dean of the Faculty of History, Literature and Human Sciences at the National University of Rwanda when the book was published.

The book *Histoire du Christianisme au Rwanda: Des Origines à nos Jours* (meaning "History of Christianity in Rwanda, from the Beginning Up to Date"), written under the direction of Tharcisse Gatwa and Laurent Rutinduka, was another key work used. The book was helpful in knowing how Christianity was introduced and spread in Rwanda, as well as presenting the negative approach of the first Western missionaries towards Rwandan culture.

Bigirumwami emerged in this period during which Rwandan culture was considered as evil and inferior to Western culture. Did he also adopted the Western perceptive and spread the gospel while opposing it to Rwandan culture? The next chapters, especially the third, will explore this question and other asked questions.

1

Western Missionaries Perceptions of the Pre-Colonial Rwandan Worldview and Its Impact

Introduction

THIS CHAPTER DEALS WITH history of Rwanda as the setting for Bigirumwami's life and work. The history of Rwanda can be divided into many periods, but three major periods are mainly used: pre-colonial, colonial, and post-colonial. Currently, a fourth period could be identified, the post–Tutsi genocide period. This chapter will focus on Rwandan primal religion in pre-colonial Rwandan society and in colonial Rwanda, focusing on the process of Christianizing Rwanda and its effects. This historical background will help in understanding the context in which Bigirumwami emerged.

Pre-Colonial Rwanda

The history of Rwanda holds many controversies. During December 14–18, 1998, the National University of Rwanda through the Faculty of History, Literature and Human Sciences organized an international seminar to discuss these controversies. Discussing the topic presented during the seminar, Byanafashe Déogratias clarified that "Les différentes présentations portaient sur les sujets de l'histoire du Rwanda parce que nous considérons que, de ce fait, ce sont des sujets sensibles à la falsification"[1] ["The various presentations dealt with these topics of Rwandan history because we consider that, for this reason, they are susceptible to falsification"]. These controversial topics covered six themes: (1) "Les problèmes de méthodologie et de chronologie" [The problems of methodology and chronology]; (2) "Les considérations sur le peuplement» [Considerations on settlement] ; (3) «L'Etat-Nation et les frontières» [The nation-state and the borders]; (4) «Les relations traditionnelles entre rwandais» [The traditional relations among Rwandans] ; (5) «Le phénomène colonial et d'évangélisation» [The colonial phenomenon and evangelization]; (6) «Les changements politiques et leur nature, Enfin le Génocide et les Rescapés de 1994» [The political changes and their nature, finally the genocide and the survivors of 1994].[2]

Pre-Colonial Rwandan Society

Before the Nyiginya Clan dominated other clans and formed the Kingdom of Rwanda in 1312, starting with Ruganzu I Bwimba,[3] there were many kingdoms led by clans around the region. These kingdoms included: Enengwe Kingdom; Singa Kangdom; the northern kingdom was Bugoyi; the central kingdom was Nduga; the eastern kingdom was Kinyaga; and the southern kingdoms were Burwi, Baanda Kingdom, Oongera Kingdom, the Ziggaba Kingdom, Gesera Kingdom, and the Gara Kingdom.[4] In defining Rwanda, Muzungu Bernardin wrote, "Le Rwanda est une réalité humaine, sociale et géographique"[5] [Rwanda is a human, social, and geographical reality]. In ancient Rwanda, the family was the pillar, as Rwanda was conceived as "one big family." The individual

---

1. Byanafashe, «Présentation,» 7.
2. Byanafashe, «Présentation,» 7.
3. Muzungu, *Histoire du Rwanda Précolonial*, 103–4.
4. Muzungu, *Histoire du Rwanda Précolonial*, 62–71.
5. Muzungu, *Histoire du Rwanda Précolonial*, 53.

identity was not separated from parents, lineage, clan, and place.[6] Muzungu gives a good example from the genealogies list:

> Sendashonga (nom individuel) wa Sebagangari (Fils de Sebagangari), Umunyiginya (nom du clan) w'Umuhindiro (nom du lignage) wo muri Nyaruguru (nom de la région qu'il habitait), i Runyinya (nom de la colline où se situait sa résidence).[7]

> [Sendashonga (individual name) wa Sebagangari (son of Sebagangari), Umunyiginya (clan name) w'Umuhindiro (lineage name) wo muri Nyaruguru (name of the region where he lived), i Runyinya (name of the hill on which his resident was located).]

From the above example, we may understand how a Rwandan was not an isolated individual, but rather he/she was part of one big family. Another important element is that at no point did social classes from that time (Tutsi, Hutu, and Twa) changed into separate ethnic groups as promoted during the colonial period are mentioned. The name of the Tutsi class is only mentioned during the presentation of the genealogy of Rwandan kings. From Alexis Kagame, we may take one example: "*Yuhi ni uwa KIGELI, izina lye ali Umututsi akaba RWABUGIRI, Nyina ni NYIRAKIGELI, izina lye ari Umututsi akaba MURORUNKWERE, . . . Akaba umukobwa w'Abakono, . . . Ahoga nyine, Abakono bakabyarana Abami n'Abanyiginya!*"[8] [Yuhi is son of KIGELI, His name when he was a Tutsi is RWABUGIRI, his mother is NYIRAKIGELI, her name when she was a Tutsi is MURORUNKWERE . . . she is a daughter of Abakono . . . therefore, the Abakono give birth to the kings with Abanyiginya]. Kagame indicates that in ancient Rwanda every king had his Tutsi name and after enthronement he was given a royal name.[9] The royal name was given with a specific function[10]

6. Muzungu, *Histoire du Rwanda Précolonial*, 53.

7. Muzungu, *Histoire du Rwanda Précolonial*, 53.

8. Kagame, *Inganji Kalinga*, 107–8.

9. Kagame, *Inganji Kalinga*, 122.

10. Muzungu, *Histoire du Rwanda Précolonial*, 152–53.

and it was an indication that the king was elevated above classes. By becoming a king, he was no longer seen as a human being. Rwandan kings were seen as divine kings; this is the reason why it was said "*Umwami avukana imbuto*,"[11] meaning "The king is born with seed." This was an indication that the king was chosen before his birth and therefore he was set apart from classes at his enthronement. For *Umugabekazi*, meaning "queen mother," two names were mentioned: the royal name and the Tutsi name; and her clan was mentioned because few clans were considered as *Ibibanda*.[12] The *Ibibanda* were the matri-dynasty clans, which were allowed to marry with the Abanyiginya dynasty. *Umugabekazi* was the second important person after the king; she was the one to rule when the enthroned king was a child.

On describing pre-colonial Rwandan society, Muzungu continues by indicating that "les alliances matrimoniales, les structures sociales, militaires et administrative, les droits et les devoirs socio-économiques, tous ces aspects de la vie humaine étaient régis dans et par le cadre familial"[13] [Matrimonial alliances, social, military and administrative structures, rights and socio-economic duties, all these aspects of human life were governed in and by the family]. Muzungu gave a summary of how the pre-colonial Rwandan extended family was structured: (1) hearth = *Urugo*, (2) lineage = *Inzu*, (3) clan = *Ubwoko*, (4) the country = *Igihugu*.[14] *Umwami*, meaning "king," was considered as the father of the big family (kingdom) and Rwandans as his children. The monarch lived for his people to the extent of dying for them.[15] There was no individual life or separation of individuals and their geographical location. Pre-colonial Rwanda was a big family, headed by *Umwami*.

11. Muzungu, *Histoire du Rwanda Précolonial*, 90.

12. From the list of queen mother by Muzungu we notice that the following clans were the only ones considered as *ibibanda*: Zigaaba, Siinga, Eega, Ha, Kono, Gesera. Muzungu, *Histoire du Rwanda Précolonial*, 98–99.

13. Muzungu, *Histoire du Rwanda Précolonial*, 53.

14. Muzungu, *Histoire du Rwanda Précolonial*, 54–59.

15. Muzungu, *Histoire du Rwanda Précolonial*, 59.

Religion in Pre-Colonial Rwanda

"Religion" may have different meanings due to the fact that people may have different ways of defining it. I define "religion" as the relationship between human beings and God the creator of the world or the gods that they believe in. In term of religion, our Rwandan ancestors left behind a huge legacy for the contemporary generation. What follows will clearly show that Rwandans had an elevated concept of God, in spite of what the early missionaries thought, and that Bigirumwami saw this clearly.

The Concept of Imana in Pre-Colonial Rwanda

There is a famous Rwandan proverb that says, "*Imana yirirwa ahandi, igataha i Rwanda*" ("God spends the day elsewhere and spends the night in Rwanda").[16] Literally, it means "Rwanda is God's home," but the true meaning of the saying is "However hard, everything gets better at the end of the day."[17] Banyarwanda had and still has a strong belief in the existence of *Imana rurema*, God the creator of everything. Defining the word, Alexandre Kimenyi writes that:

> The Kinyarwanda word *Imana* written as such but pronounced [*imaana*], since the official orthography doesn't mark tones and long vowels, is polysemous and has 10 distinct meanings (Irenée Jacob, 1980). These different denotations from the same lexical item are metonymically related. An association or factual contiguity exists among all these meanings. The first referent is God. The second meaning is chance or good luck. Others refer to (i) animals used for divination such as cow, sheep, chicks, or any other object used for this purpose such as animal fat, dices, etc.[18]

---

16. Sibo, *Imigani y'Ikinyarwanda*, 31.
17. Sibo, *Imigani y'Ikinyarwanda*, 31.
18. Kimenyi, "Imana in Rwanda."

The word *Imana* had and still has many meanings, but they can be summarized into three: *Imana* as Creator, *Imana* as luck, and *Imana* as response and tools used in divination.

Imana Rurema, "God the Creator"

For Jacques Delforge, the Barundi and the Banyarwanda venerate *Imana* in the same way that the Basiba venerate *Rugaba*, Supreme God, Creator of the universe, and Supreme Benefactor, but without ever making sacrifices to him.[19] To *Imana*, too, sacrifices are never made; no prayers are addressed to him, much like an inaccessible superior being.[20] For Rwandans *Imana* is remote; he is not a human being, for he doesn't need anything from humans as he is the owner of everything. This explains why Rwandans say "*Imana iraguha, ntimugura, iyo muguze iraguhenda*" [*Imana* gives (things) to you (for free), you don't buy from him, when you trade with him, he becomes very expensive or Imana (God) provides for free, you don't buy from him, when you do it cost you]. The saying may also mean, "God's gift has no appeal."[21] For Rwandans, trying to give something to God is like investing where you will not gain profit; there is no need. "There is no necessity to gather together, to pray to him, to worship him, to thank him, to have holy days, holy places and holy books in his name. He doesn't need any of this. There is thus no need for proselytism or conversion because each individual is aware of his existence."[22] The pre-colonial Rwandan concept of *Imana* was not far from the Christian concept of God. Kimenyi indicates that "*Imana* is very much similar to the Christian God. He is the Creator of everything, he is Almighty, He knows everything, and He is everywhere. He loves his creation; He loves everybody and doesn't discriminate."[23] We may ask how

19. Delforge, *Rwanda Tel Qu'Ils L'Ont Vu*, 41–52.
20. Delforge, *Rwanda Tel Qu'Ils L'Ont Vu*, 41–52.
21. Sibo, *Imigani y'Ikinyarwanda*, 31.
22. Kimenyi, "Imana in Rwanda."
23 Kimenyi, "Language, Names and Religious Beliefs."

Rwandans were aware of the existence of *Imana* when there was no gathering or sacrifices for *Imana*. Different ways may help us to understand how Rwandans were able to know *Imana*.

Proverbs

Rwandans have many proverbs related to *Imana*. "*Imana igira amaboko maremare*"[24] [God has long arms, or God will get to you wherever you are]. The proverb shows that Rwandans were aware of the omnipotence of God, who is able to reach everyone wherever he or she is. Another proverb says, "*Imana ntigira umuryango*," meaning God doesn't have a family. The proverb also means that "God is impartial, he neither takes sides nor favours some individuals over others."[25] For Rwandans, the fact that God does not have a family was important as it shows that he cannot be partisan because he doesn't belong to any particular family. Rwandan proverbs that illustrate their perceptions towards *Imana* are many.[26]

The proverbs reveal in a remarkable way how Rwandans were aware of the existence of *Imana* and the role he plays in their lives. They knew that they cannot influence *Imana* and that *Imana* is not going to be the one to push them to act. They have to work and wait for *ubushake bw'Imana*, meaning "the will of God."

Names Given to Imana

Imana wasn't the only name given to God in pre-Christian Rwanda. There were other names given to *Imana*, which portray how

---

24. Sibo, *Imigani y'Ikinyarwanda*, 31.

25 Kimenyi, "Language, Names and Religious Beliefs."

26 Some other proverbs from Kimenyi: *Abagiye inama, Imana irabasanga*; "Those who consult each other are joined by Imana." He also wants human beings to be active and responsible. *Imana ifasha abifashije*; "Imana helps those who can help themselves." *Imana ihora ihoze*; "God takes revenge without having to hurry." *Imana itanga ishaka*; "God gives when he wants." Kimenyi, "Language, Names and Religious Beliefs."

they conceived Him. Below are some other names of *Imana* and their meanings according to Kimenyi:

> *Nyagasani (nyagasani)* /*nya+a+ka+sani*/ means 'the one who has luck'. *Rugira (rugirá)* from the verb *kugira* signifies 'the one who causes everything or the owner of everything'. *Rurema* /*ru-rem-a*/ means the creator. *Iyakare (iyakare)/iya+kare/* means 'that of early' or 'of times immemorial'. This implies that God is 'ancient' or the oldest being. Iyambere (iyaambere) /*iya+imbere*/ 'the one of before'. The name implies that God was the first to exist and that he preceded everything.[27]

The meaning of the names shows clearly how Rwandans had a strong conviction in *Imana*. They knew that he is the Creator who existed before all things. Many researchers have shown that the mentioned theophoric names were all pre-Christianity. In his article, "Immana [*sic*] y'I Rwanda," meaning "God Who Reigns in Rwanda," Muzungu Bernardin gives a long list of all pre-Christian Rwandan theophoric names.[28] In justifying his research, Muzungu points out that there are some theophoric names that were to be examined and confirmed if they were used in traditional Rwanda or pre-Christian Rwanda.[29] All theophoric names given above are pre-Christianity as they are on the list given by Muzungu.

Names Given to People

Kwita Izina, which means naming a child, or *guterura umwana*,[30] meaning holding a child, was one of the important rites in pre-colonial Rwanda that is not given much attention today. The rite of *kwita izina* had to be carried out and the name that was given had significance. Here are some Rwandan names that carry their beliefs and understanding of *Imana*:

27. Kimenyi, "Language, Names and Religious Beliefs."
28. Muzungu, "Immana y'I Rwanda."
29. Muzungu, "Immana y'I Rwanda," 4.
30. Bigirumwami, *Imihango*, 73.

Habarugira 'The Causer of everything [that] exists', *Habiyakare* 'The Early [one to] exist', *Habiyambere* 'The First One [to] exist', *Nsengiyaremye* 'I pray to the Creator', *Ndagijimana* 'God is my shepherd', *Harerimana* 'Only God educates', *Mukeshimana* 'I owe him/her to God', *Musabyimana* 'I asked him/her from God', *Havugimana* 'Only God speaks', . . .[31]

We may ask how Rwandans were able to give their children names about prayer and praise when they had no worship and praise reserved for *Imana*. In reading Bishop Aloys Bigirumwami's book *Imihango, n'Imigenzo, n'Imiziririzo mu Rwanda*, translated into English as "Traditions, Rites, and Taboos in Rwanda," he never mentions traditions or rites involving prayers or worship to *Imana* in "*kuraguza*[32] divination "*Guterekera*"[33] offering to ghosts, and "*Kubandwa* cult."[34] The names related to praise and prayers were more noticeable after the spread of Christianity in Rwanda. If *Imana* was considered to be far from humans, to whom were Rwandans expected to offer drinks and food, and why? To whom were they to present their requests? In analyzing the second meaning of *Imana* used in divination as *Imana yeze*, we will get answers to these questions.

Imana yeze, *"Divine Response"*

Imana was untouchable and unseen for Rwandans; therefore, his power and presence could be felt among some objects and some ancestors' ghosts. An *imana* was also an object or animal that was brought to *Umupfumu*, the diviner, by someone who wanted to find out the answer to his/her request. If the response was positive, the diviner would indicate: "*Imana yeze*." According to Bigirumwami:

---

31. Kimenyi, "Imana in Rwanda."
32. Bigirumwami, *Imihango, n'Imigenzo*, 219–52.
33. Bigirumwami, *Imihango, n'Imigenzo*, 252–70.
34. Bigirumwami, *Imihango, n'Imigenzo*, 270–323.

Quand on dit *"Imana yeze"* : Dieu blanc, (2) Dieu favorable, on pourrait aussi bien traduire : sort favorable. Il ne faut prendre cette expression au sens littéral, c'est plutôt une allégorie. On n'aimera pas dire « *nambaye inka yeze* » je porte sur moi une vache blanche ; on dira plutôt : je porte Imana qui m'est toujours favorable.[35]

[When one says *"Imana yeze"*: White God (2), Favourable God, one could also translate: favourable fate. This expression should not be taken literally, but rather an allegory. One will not like to say *"nambaye inka yeze"* I carry on me a white cow; they say: I wear *Imana*, which always favors me.]

Imana is used here as an answer given. Concerning why the title *Imana* is applied to things, Bishop Bigirumwami clarifies that it is not uncommon to apply the title of *Imana* to things that are found to be perfect. Thus, of a ficus, in Kinyarwanda *umusene*, or of a good, gentle, benevolent, wise man, one says: *"Ni Imana y'i Rwanda"* (it is God very good). This is equivalent to saying in French: *"C'est la bonté même,"* meaning, it is goodness itself.[36] *Imana* in divination was applied but with a different meaning: *Imana* had the meaning of a good person or things, sacred, and a favorable fate.

Imana *as Luck*

The third way in which the word *Imana* was used was when a Rwandan wanted to indicate that someone is lucky. They said *"Kugira Imana,"* literally meaning "to have God," but in reality they wanted to explain that she/he is blessed. *"Ugira Imana kuba ugeze aha amahoro"* literally implies "You have God for reaching here peacefully"; the actual meaning is "You are blessed for reaching here without trouble on the way." Another expression used is *"Ugira Imana wowe abana barakumvira."* It literally means "Children obey you since you have God"; the actual meaning is "You are

---

35. Bigirumwami, *Imihango, n'Imigenzo*, annex, 16.
36. Bigirumwami, *Imihango, n'Imigenzo*, annex, 16.

blessed that children obey you." For Rwandan luck, *amahirwe*, is not a fate but blessings derived from God, therefore *Kugira Imana*, meaning to have God, doesn't mean that someone has God ontologically but that he/she is blessed, lucky.

The Mediators

The conception of *Imana* made pre-colonial Rwandans look for mediators between them and *Imana* because *Imana* was considered to be supreme and not a human being. It was not possible for Rwandans to have direct relationship with *Imana*. Muzungu indicates that the ancestors and the society were the mediators.[37] With *Imana* being invisible, the dead became the mediators, hence the cult to ancestors. For Muzungu, "le culte des ancêtres au Rwanda se présente sous deux formes, *Guterekera* et *Kubandwa*. Le premier s'adresse aux ancêtres 'naturels', c'est-à-dire aux parents défunt tandis que le second s'adresse aux ancêtres 'adoptives', à savoir les '*Imandwa*' venus de la secte de Ryangombe."[38] [Ancestor worship in Rwanda comes in two forms, *Guterekera* and *Kubandwa*. The first is addressed to the "natural" ancestors that are to the deceased parents, while the second addresses the "adoptive" ancestors, namely the "*Imandwa*" from the Ryangombe sect.] Concerning the society as mediator, Muzungu indicates that it was not the whole society but the political authorities like *Umwami* (king) who were considered to have divine mandate.[39]

From the discussion above, we can conclude that Rwandans were aware of the existence of *Imana* the Creator, the Almighty, who owns everything. They knew that *Imana* doesn't have a wife and that he is beyond gender; he is not a human being as he doesn't even have a family. Through their proverbs, names, and folklore tales, it is easy to notice pre-colonial Rwandans' strong belief in

---

37. Muzungu, *Histoire du Rwanda Précolonial*, 314.
38. Muzungu, *Histoire du Rwanda Précolonial*, 314.
39. Muzungu, *Histoire du Rwanda Précolonial*, 314.

Imana; ancestors and society authorities like the king were the mediators between Rwandan and Imana.

Colonization of Rwanda and the Spread of Christianity in Rwanda

The Rwandan Kingdom officially became a German colony in 1897[40] and Germany colonized Rwanda from 1897 to 1916. During the First World War in 1916, Germans were defeated in Rwanda and Belgians took over and colonized Rwanda through three phases (the military occupation from 1916 to 1926, the mandate period from 1926 to 1946, and the trusteeship period from 1946 to 1962).[41]

Western Missionaries in Rwanda

In Rwanda, colonizers and Western missionaries did not arrive at the same time. German colonizers were the first to arrive and the first missionaries followed them. We will focus on Christian missionaries, especially Roman Catholic and Protestants. We will consider the Muslims who arrived in Rwanda in 1910.[42]

Roman Catholic Missionaries

The first Christian missionaries to arrive in Rwanda were the Roman Catholic missionaries headed by Bishop Joseph Hirth in 1900. On February 2, 1900, they were able to meet King Yuhi V Musinga at Nyanza. Rwanda and her entire population had their

---

40. Repubulika y'u Rwanda Perezidansi ya Repubulika, *Ubumwe Bw'Abanyarwanda*, 13.

41. Repubulika y'u Rwanda Perezidansi ya Repubulika, *Ubumwe Bw'Abanyarwanda*, 14–16.

42. Repubulika y'u Rwanda Perezidansi ya Repubulika, *Ubumwe Bw'Abanyarwanda*, 16.

traditional understanding of God[43] when missionaries arrived. The Roman Catholic missionaries started the evangelization of Rwanda, and "the motivation was to occupy the country before the arrival of Protestants and Muslims."[44] On February 8, 1900, Save the First Mission was founded and Zaza, Nyundo, Rwaza, Mibilizi, and Kabgayi were founded between 1900 and 1906.[45] Although the Roman Catholics wanted the occupation of the country within a short period, Rutinduka points out that between 1900 and 1917 the evangelization was not successful.[46] The main reason for the lack of success was the refusal of King Yuhi V Musinga to convert to Christianity. When Roman Catholic missionaries arrived the main target was to start evangelizing within the ruling class. Rutinduka indicates that the resistance of King Yuhi V Musinga to convert to Christianity was one of the major obstacles that the Roman Catholics faced in the course of Christianizing Rwanda.[47]

When the Belgians colonizers arrived, they were also displeased with King Yuhi V Musinga, who had been working well with the Germans, so the Catholic missionaries took the opportunity to lead the deposition of Yuhi V Musinga in November 1931.[48] According to Bishop Léon Paul Classe, he had to be dethroned and driven out Rwanda because he prevented his people from being baptized for the salvation of their souls.[49] Dethroning King Yuhi V Musinga was the only way Rwandans could be saved according to Roman Catholic missionaries. King Yuhi V Musinga was replaced by his son, King Mutara III Rudahigwa, who accepted to convert to Christianity. In the history of the expansion of the Christian

---

43. Rutinduka, "L'Église catholique au Rwanda," 15.

44. Rutinduka, "L'Église catholique au Rwanda," 16.

45. Rutinduka, "L'Église catholique au Rwanda," 16.

46. Rutinduka, "L'Église catholique au Rwanda," 17.

47. King Yuhi V Musinga and the great chiefs of Rwanda like Kabare, Ruhinankiko, Cyitatira, Mpamarugamba, and other dignitaries didn't want to see the shining of the Catholic Church. They were afraid to see themselves one day pushed aside by the foreign whites, who were systematically occupying the country. Rutinduka, "L'Église catholique au Rwanda," 17.

48. Rutinduka, "L'Église catholique au Rwanda," 22.

49. Rutinduka, "L'Église catholique au Rwanda," 22.

faith, Andrew F. Walls indicates that there were commonalities and differences with respect to the conversions of nations.[50] As the use of nobility made it possible for the Christian faith to spread fast in Northwest Europe, especially among the English and Franks, so the conversion of Mutara III Rudahigwa also made it possible for Christianity to spread fast in Rwanda. Seeing how his father was dethroned, Mutara III Rudahigwa chose to be allies with Roman Catholic missionaries, who had been instrumental in deposition of his father. Thus, what took place in Rwanda was similar to the outcomes of the conversion of Clovis[51] and Edwin[52] in early Northwest Europe. There were mass conversions, which made it possible for Christianity to become the state religion to the point that Rwanda was called a "Christian Kingdom."[53] It is noteworthy to point out that the arrival of different Protestant missionaries in Rwanda motivated the Roman Catholic missionaries to play a role in the dethronement of King Yuhi V Musinga, as they wanted to

---

50. Walls, *Missionary Movement in Christian History*, 68–69.

51. The conversion of King Clovis has been and is still a historical debate. About the debate, William M. Daly indicates that for Tessier he "infers that Clovis's motives probably included both political sagacity and religious inclination." He continues and indicates that "Lucien Musset's view is little different from Tessier's. Yet, while common denominators of a new portrait have thus emerged in France, the old one can still resurface." Apart, Tessier and Musset, Daly indicates that other authors also have different views about Clovis's conversion. They agree that: "[H]is choice of Catholic orthodoxy over Arianism enabled him to organize and integrate Gallo–Roman and Germanic traditions toward useful political and social ends of lasting impact on European history. While all of them recognize that such pragmatic reasons lay behind his conversion, some also allow him authentic personal conviction."Though people debated and are still debating on King Clovis's motif for conversion, they do not disagree on the fact that his conversion had an impact on his people and his kingdom in general. Daly, "Clovis," 619–20.

52. King Edwin's conversion and baptism was followed by a mass conversion starting with the nobility and then all the people of his kingdom. Paulinus became a public preacher and spent months in the kingdom baptizing people. Church buildings were built throughout the kingdom with the support of King Edwin. Bede, *History of the English Church*, 128–30.

53. Rutayisire, "Le Catholicisme Rwandais," 257.

convert many Rwandans using the son of Yuhi V, who was already a Roman Catholic convert.

Protestant Missionaries

On the side of Protestatant missionaries, the Lutheran missionaries headed by Ernst Johanssen and Gerhard Ruccius, with some Tanzanian evangelists, were the first to arrive in Rwanda in 1907. They established the first missionary station at Zinga. When German missionaries had to leave the country during the First World War, stations such as Rubengera, Kirinda, and Remera-Rukoma were established.[54] In the same vein and with the support of Belgian authorities, La Société Belge de Missions Protestantes au Congo (SBMPC) in 1921[55] took over the mission stations established by German Lutherans and continued the evangelization in Rwanda by Presbyterians. Other Protestant missionaries to arrive were the Seventh Day Adventists in 1919[56] and the Anglican missionary of Church Missionary Society (CMS) in 1920.[57] The Danish Baptist Mission, the first Baptist mission in Rwanda, arrived in 1939.[58] The Pentecostal mission entered the course of spreading Christianity in Rwanda by the arrival of La Mission Libre Suédoise (MLS) in 1940.[59] In 1942, Methodist Mission also arrived in Rwanda.[60] These Protestant missionaries arrived in Rwanda during the colonial period and met the Catholic missionaries' influence.[61]

54. Gatwa, "L'Église Presbytérienne au Rwanda," 63–75.

55. Gatwa, "L'Église Presbytérienne au Rwanda," 75.

56. Birikunzira, "L'Église Adventiste du 7e Jour au Rwanda," 101–2.

57. Kalimba, "L'Église Anglicane au Rwanda," 119.

58. Rugambage, «L'Union des Églises Baptistes au Rwanda,» 148–49.

59. Habarurema, "L'Église Pentecôte au Rwanda, 177–78.

60. Niyikiza, "L'Église Méthodiste au Rwanda,» 162–63.

61. For Catholic missionaries, Rwanda was their territory; therefore they felt attacked on their own territory by the arrival of Protestants. This competitive spirit marked the evangelization of Rwanda, and became one of the major factors that led to discrimination and divisions among Rwandans, firstly based on religious denominations and secondly on ethnic groups.

While the Catholic missionaries were focusing mostly on acquiring many members, Bible translation became one of the Protestant missionaries' priorities. The first German missionaries started the work in 1911 and other missionaries followed and finished it.

In 1957, the whole Bible in Kinyarwada, *Bibiliya Yera*, was published.[62] For Roman Catholic missionnaires, Bible translation was not their priority; Jean Van Der Meersch, quoted by Gabriel Akimana, describes it as, "On craignait de répandre la Bible dans le peuple à cause des abus, réels ou supposés qu'en avaient fait les réformateurs. [They were afraid of distributing the Bible among the people because of real or assumed abuses that the reformers had made of it.]"[63] It was in 1990,[64] some ninety years after they first arrived in Rwanda, that the whole Roman Catholic Bible, *Bibiliya Ntagatifu*,[65] meaning "Holy Bible," was published.

Western Missionary Perception of Rwandan Religion

The arrival of Western missionaries in Rwanda led to many political, economical, and sociocultural changes. This section examines how the missionaries conceived Rwandan primal religion when they arrived in Rwanda. There was incomprehension in the European missionaries' encounter with Rwandan primal religions. Concerning the Western missionaries incomprehension of the primal religions of other civilizations outside Europe, Gillian Mary Bediako points out that apart from the influence of Christendom, "one may suggest, therefore, that the 'fog of incomprehension' in the European encounter with primal religion has also to be accounted for by a suppression of the primal religious memory and world view, in the process of the Christianization of Europe."[66] In

---

62. Akimana, "Translation Issues," 92–100.

63. Akimana, "Translation Issues," 100.

64. Akimana, "Translation Issues," 106.

65. Akimana, "Translation Issues," 106.

66. Bediako, *Primal Religion and the Bible*, 65.

Rwanda, according to Christopher C. Taylor, "As Christian evangelization progressed, Catholic missionaries substituted the idea of the Judeo–Christian God for the Rwandan idea of "diffuse fecundating fluid," while retaining the term, *imaana* [*sic*], in Bibles translated into Kinyarwanda."[67] The Roman Catholic missionaries did not use the word *Imana* when they arrived in Rwanda. For them, *Imana* was not the Supreme God; they considered *Imana* as *Imana*, a god. As Westermann Diedrich points out in describing the first missionary's impressions of Africans:

> We are possessed by such an unbounded feeling of superiority, and are so unable to understand and appreciate anything not of our own kind, that we consider the annihilation of the social and mental world of a continent as benefit and a blessing for its inhabitants. We do not take into account that the African has evolved a genius of his own. There is an African state of mind, an African view of things, an African material and mental culture.[68]

Due to missionaries' feelings of superiority and their estimation of Rwandans as inferior, they were not able to understand that *Imana* was not simply a deity for Rwandans. In the first written history of Rwanda, Pagès describes Rwandans regarding their religion:

> Au point de vue religieux le Munyarwanda est superstitieux a l'excès. Il reconnait l'existence d'un être suprême (Imana), créateur de toutes choses, mais ne s'en occupe pas beaucoup dans la pratique de la vie, pour la raison qu'il ne fait pas de mal. Ses soins vont aux mânes qu'il redoute. Il croit, en effet, que les esprits des morts sont les auteurs des maux qui l'affligent. De là les invocations, des offrandes, des libations devant l'édicule forme capuchon, où se localise l'esprit irrité qu'on lui a signalé. Le Munyarwanda est assujetti à la loi des Tabous (imiziro).[69]

---

67. Taylor, "Kings and Chaos in Rwanda," 41–58.

68. Westermann, Value of the Africa's Past," 418–19.

69. Pagès, *Un Royaume Hamite*, 55.

[From a religious point of view, Munyarwanda is super-stitious to excess. He recognizes the existence of a su-preme being (Imana), creator of all things, but does not deal much with it in the practice of life, for the reason that he does no harm. His devotion goes to the spirits he dreads. He believes, indeed, that the spirits of the dead are the authors of the evils which afflict him. From there the invocations, the offerings, the libations before the cup-shaped cup, where is located the irritated spirit that was pointed out to him. The Munyarwanda is subject to the law of Taboo (imiziro).]

In describing Munyarwanda's religion, Pagès directly reveals out his superiority complex. For him, "Munyarwanda is supersti-tious to excess,"; he does not indicate whom he was comparing him with. In his description, it appears that to Munyarwanda the spirit of the dead was just the author of the evil that affects him/her. How come, then, the same spirit was taken by Munyarwanda as the mediator between him/her and *Imana*? Yet in their belief God was not a source of evil; some *Bazimu* spirits of the dead were the source of evils, but not all spirits of the dead were seen as such. It was not possible for missionaries to accept the fact that those whom they considered as pagan and uncivilized may have known God, which is the reason why Pagès assumes Munyar-wanda to be superstitious. Concerning *Imana* and missionaries' views, Rutayisire indicates that:

La place de Dieu (Imana) a été particulièrement source de conflit entre les missionnaires et les autochtones. Les missionnaires étaient convaincus qu'il était impos-sible aux « sauvages » d'acquérir une idée convenable de la « vraie divinité ». Ils n'admettaient que des puissances mystérieuses. Le terme « Imana » était pour eux impro-pre a designer le Dieu de la Bible, ceci d'autres plus qu'il avait de multiple sens . . . Les premiers missionnaires du Rwanda et du Burundi n'ont pas compris les différents sens d'Imana dans le contexte culturel. Ils s'en sont méfiés et ont imposé un mot swahili, moins souillé pour eux, celui de « Mungu ».[70]

[The place of God (*Imana*) was particularly a source of conflict between the missionaries and the natives. The missionaries were convinced that it was impossible for the "savages" to acquire a proper idea of the "true divinity." They admitted only mysterious powers. The term "*Imana*" was unfit for them to designate the God of the Bible, all the more so because he had multiple meanings . . . The first missionaries of Rwanda and Burundi did not understand the different meanings of *Imana* in the cultural context. They mistrusted them and imposed a Swahili word, less soiled for them, that of "*Mungu*" (in certain early texts "*Mulungu*").]

Why the use of Swahili or Luganda words, instead of using Kinyarwanda? Muzungu indicates that:

La providence a voulu que dans ce changement de nom, les Rwandais remarquent que le christianisme est un message d'une extraordinaire nouveauté, et que le danger de syncrétisme avec leur religion païenne soit largement écarté.[71]

[Providence desired that through this change of name Rwandans should notice that Christianity is an extraordinarily novel message, and that the danger of syncretism with their pagan religion should be widely rejected.]

For Muzungu, missionaries wanted to avoid syncretism, but he further points out the negative impact of using *Mungu* in the place of *Imana*: "L'inconvénient de ce changement a été que « Mungu » est resté un Dieu étranger" [The disadvantage of this change was that "*Mungu*" remained a foreign God]. The competitive spirit between Roman Catholic missionaries and Protestant missionaries was another reason for the use of a blank slate method towards Rwandan culture. There was no time for the Western missionaries

---

70. Rutayisire, «Catholicisme Rwandais,» 259.

71. Muzungu, "Imana y'i Rwanda," 2.

to study Rwandan society and understand it. It was only later that some missionaries and Rwandans like Bigirumwami,[72] Kagame Alexis,[73] and Muzungu Bernardin,[74] started to point out the danger of Westernization of Rwandans.

Due to resistance from Rwandans who continued to use the term *Imana*, and research results of local Rwandans, the Roman Catholic missionaries finally agreed to use the term *Imana* in the Bible and their preaching.[75] According to Priest Muzungu Bernardin, Bishop Bigirumwami played a remarkable role on the side of Roman Catholic Church to accept the use of *Imana* instead of *Mungu* in masses and in their Bible, which was in the process of translation.[76]

The relationship of Roman Catholic missionaries with Rwandan culture and with primal religions has been one of conflict.[77] It may be good to point out that not all missionaries had negative views toward Africans, Rwandans, and their culture. In his work "Is Pagan Dead? The Theological Legacy of Protestant Missionaries to Rwanda," Gerard van't Spijker examined the work of Ernst Johanssen in Rwanda. For Johanssen, Africans had an idea of religion and he did not agree with the mainstream colonialists' idea, which portrayed Africans as having no idea of religion.[78] His greatest achievement was to avoid both the spirit of superiority and the approach of researchers of ethnology and cultural anthropology who considered Africans as "primitive men" that they had to investigate. "Johanssen opposes himself to the evolutionary concept of religion of the specialists of the History of Religion of his time."[79] This helped Johanssen to value

---

72. Bigirumwami, *Imana y'Abantu.*

73. Kagame, *Philosophie bantu-rwandaise de l'être.*

74. Muzungu, "Imana y'i Rwanda."

75. Rutayisire, «Catholicisme Rwandais,» 259.

76. Bernardin Muzungu, conversation, July 9, 2018, Kigali.

77. Rutayisire, «Catholicisme Rwandais,» 258.

78. Spijker, "Is Pagan Dead?," 3.

79. Spijker, "Is Pagan Dead?," 3–4.

some aspects of Rwandan primal religion to the point that he advocated for inculturation. Spijker indicates that:

> This missionary approach of Johanssen has resulted in the collection of a great number of myths and fairy tales, expressions and proverbs of Rwandan culture. In the Reader for schools at the mission stations, printed under the name *Ifiberi* in 1911, several of these tales and myths were reproduced. A second result is the creation of a Church language close to the Rwandan imaginary world, with words taken from everyday life: *Imana* for God, *Umwuka Wera,* for Holy Ghost, *Itorero* for Church. The intention to create church ceremonies inspired by Rwandan costumes, for instance rituals around marriage, was not realized, due to the fact the German Lutheran missionaries did not have the time to create vital Christian communities, by the time they were forced to leave the scene in 1916.[80]

Johanssen's missionary approach explains why he and his colleague were the first to start the translation of the Bible into Kinyarwanda. The other Protestant missionaries who arrived after the German missionaries did not follow in the footsteps of the German Lutheran missionaries under Johanssen's leadership. Spijker indicates that "The most elaborate reflection on the relationship between African traditional beliefs and practices and Christianity is that of Ernst Johanssen. As Johanssen had to leave the country untimely [*sic*], his ideas were not applied to the missionary work in Rwanda."[81] Other Protestant missionaries who came after the Lutheran missionaries continued to exhibit the mentality of superiority opposed to inferiority, and demonized everything related to Rwandan culture. In contrast, Roman Catholic missionaries began to have a positive attitude towards Rwandan primal religions after Vatican II. It was not only the Western missionaries who were influenced by Vatican II, but also Rwandans like Bigirumwami.[82]

---

80. Spijker, "Is Pagan Dead?," 5.
81. Spijker, "Is Pagan Dead?," 17.
82. Bigirumwami, *Umuntu*, 97.

Implications of Western Missionary Perspectives of Rwandan Primal Religion

The main method used by both Catholic and Protestant missionaries in evangelization was to make Rwandans deny their culture and accept being new creatures. Everything related to Rwandan culture was seen as evil or pagan; therefore, a Christian had to completely and publicly declare that he or she denounces all traditions and customs before being baptized. *Imana* was redefined and the word was later used, but Christians had to forget *Imana y'I Rwanda*, meaning "the God of Rwanda," who was considered an idol by missionaries. The problem is to know how Rwandans had to differentiate these two *Imana* conceptions. The refusal of missionaries to accept that *Imana Rurema*, God the Creator, whom Rwandans knew, was the same Creator God preached by Western missionaries, although Rwandans were not aware of the Trinity of the Father, Son, and Holy Spirit, is the main source of the belief that *Imana* was imported from outside of Rwanda, mostly called *Imana y'abazungu*,[83] meaning "God of white people." In 1999, the government, headed by Pasteur Bizimungu as president of Rwanda, asked a commission made up of scholars and other experienced people to conduct research on the unity

83. On the August 15, 2017, Catholic members celebrated the assumption of the Blessed Virgin Mary. On that date a man called Manirareba Herman called on Rwandans through the media not to celebrate the assumption of the Blessed Virgin Mary, but to instead celebrate the famous Rwandan queen mother and poet Nyirarumaga. According to him, Rwandans had their Imana before the arrival of white "*Abazungu*," and when they arrived they brought another God called the "God of the whites." Therefore Rwandans must stop believing in the God of the whites and go back to worshiping the Imana of their ancestors. Manirareba has already gone to court accusing Catholic Church leaders of misinterpreting the Kibeho revelations by saying that the girls received the message from the Blessed Virgin Mary; whereas, in fact, the girls had received the message from Nyirarumaga, who was telling them about what was going to happen, especially the genocide. My focus will not be on the problem of Nyirarumaga and the Blessed Virgin Mary raised by Manirareba, but rather on the "Imana y'Abazungu," God of the whites, and "Imana y'abakurambere," God of ancestors. The perception of two Imana in Rwanda is not limited to Manirareba only; it is shared by some other Rwandans.

of Rwanda before the coming of the Western colonizers and missionaires during colonization and the first republic. In the report, they pointed out that foreign religions (Christianity and Islam) played a big role in dividing Rwandans.[84] According to the report, *Imana y'i Rwanda* was ignored to the level that he disappeared from the consciousness of many people. The divisions that marked the history of Rwanda led to the genocide against Tutsi in 1994. This genocide confirmed that people didn't have *Imana* in their hearts, either the God preached by missionaries or *Imana Rurema* of ancient Rwanda. Western missionaries' perception of Rwandan primal religion led to many negative effects in Rwanda, some of which are discussed below.

The Identity Crisis

Jacques Delforge observes that:

> Ici comme partout les chrétiens auront toujours plus à souffrir que les autres ; ils sont persécutés, et par les leurs qui les appellents des traitres, et par les chefs qui craignent de perdre une partie de leur autorité, et par les voient nos chrétiens qu'avec une espèce de colère qu'ils sont impuissants à dissimuler.[85]

> [Here, as everywhere, Christians will always have more to suffer than others; they are persecuted, both by their own who call them traitors, and by the chiefs who fear to lose part of their authority, and see our Christians only with a type of anger which they are incapable of concealing.]

---

84. Republika y'u Rwanda Perezidansi ya Republika, *Ubumwe bw'Abanyarwanda*, 17. The new religions ignored the traditional religion of "Gihanga," religion of the Creator. The Catholic replaced "Imana" with "Mungu," Muslims used "Allah," and Protestants in the beginning used the word "Imana." This meant that Imana and his importance were ignored and forgotten by many people, and Imana (God) was the unifying factor, the foundation of Rwandan belief and of their living.

85. Delforge, *Rwanda Tel Qu'ils L'ont Vu*, 104.

The first Rwandan converts to Christianity were persecuted by their own people and chiefs. They were seen as traitors, *abatatiye igihango*, meaning those who have broken the covenant. To become a Christian was to deny *Imana y'I Rwanda*, the God of Rwanda; therefore, you became an enemy of Rwanda.

On the other hand, missionaries were very active in imposing Christianity without taking into consideration the Rwandan past. Kenneth Cragg sees this mission strategy as a limitation to evangelization when he writes that:

> Christianity cannot address men and ignore their gods: it may not act in the present and disown the past or wisely hold forth salvation and withhold salutation. In seeking men for Christ's sake, it is committed to the significance of all they are in their birth and their tradition, both for good or ill.[86]

Cragg presents the primal religion as part of people's life that should be given proper consideration especially in relation to or contact with Christianity. According to Cragg, people's gods and past traditions are fundamental; they are not to be ignored or directly excluded, because they form part of people's lives which have to undergo conversion to new life in Jesus.

This was not the case in Rwanda; missionaries never considered the past as relevant for Rwandans conversion, as proposed by Cragg. Therefore, the first converts stood between missionaries and Rwandan chiefs who were holding strongly to their traditional beliefs. The first converts to Christianity had to break ties with their country's traditions, rites, and customs, which put them in a similar position to the first converts to Christianity in the Roman Empire, as described by Kwame Bediako:

> An escapable element of Christian identity in the early Empire was that they were out of step with the society in general at some vital points . . . The Christians dissolved the sacred ties of customs and education, violated the religious institutions of their country, and presumptuously

---

86. Cragg, *Christianity in World Perspective*, 65.

despised whatever their fathers had believed as true, or had reverenced as sacred.[87]

The deposition of King Yuhi V Musinga led to the end of official persecution of Christians by chiefs who were without power, but in families were still being persecuted. Yuhi V was replaced by his son, Mutara III Rudahugwa, who had been baptized and accepted to offer the kingdom to the King of kings, Jesus Christ. In 1931, many Rwandans started joining the church.[88] The role of the "Bayozefite" Josephites Brothers Congregation, made up of Rwandese, *Irivuze umwami*,[89] meaning the effect of what the king says, and the Eastern African Revival played a big role in Christianizing Rwanda. Though Rwanda became a Christian kingdom after Mutara III's act of consecrating Rwanda to Jesus, the overarching pre-colonial concept of seeing Rwanda as one big family was undermined in the process, leading to the destruction of social cohesion among Rwandans.

In sum, this identity crisis was the outcome of Eurocentrism among missionaries, which caused the use of a blank slate method in the process of Christianizing Rwanda and the divide-and-rule policy. Christianity became a new identity opposed to "paganism." Therefore, Rwandans were given one choice: Christianity. This brings us to the second implication of the Western perception of Rwandan primal religion.

The Church Became a Hiding Place

The church being a hiding place is not necessarily a bad thing but it became a problem when it was made an enforced hiding place. The dethronement of King Musinga and the enthronement of Rudahigwa by missionaries was not accepted by all Rwandans, who considered Musinga as their king. They hoped he would return as some primal religious *Abapfumu* as prophets were predicting, but

87. Bediako, *Theology and Identity*, 17–18.
88. Rutinduka, «L'Église Catholique au Rwanda,» 22.
89. Rutinduka, «L'Église Catholique au Rwanda,» 22.

missionaries were clear in their answers: "Don't talk of Musinga, he is no more. Your king is Rudahigwa; don't listen to what pagans and the witches may say: 'Musinga will come back.'"[90] The resistance of some Rwandans, especially chiefs, to accepting Rudahigwa as their king shows that in the beginning Mutara III Rudahigwa was not supported as he was seen as the Western missionaries' king. The love Rwandans had for King Musinga pushed missionaries to use force in fighting against traditionalists through the practice of tabula rasa, blank slate. Rutayisire writes that:

> Les convertis devaient renoncer à leur identité culturelle et manifester un zèle dans la chasse aux signes du « paganisme ». Pour cela tous les moyens étaient bons, même les plus injustes et humuliants, pour faire « table rase » de la religion traditionelle. D'où la campagne de chasse aux sorciers et aux guérisseurs traditionnels, la destruction des amulettes et de tout ce qui était en rapport avec le culte des morts (kuragura, guterekera et kubandwa.[91]

> [The converts had to renounce their cultural identity and show a zeal in the hunt for the signs of "paganism." For all the means were good, even the most unjust and humiliating, to make a "blank slate" of traditional religion, hence the campaign of hunting the witches and traditional healers, the destruction of amulets and what was in relation to the cult of the dead (*kuragura, guterekera,* and *kubandwa*).]

Christians moved from being persecuted to actively persecuting those who were not accepting renouncement of their primal beliefs. What was done in past before the arrival of colonizers and missionaries had become outmoded and therefore not worth doing. In order to have peace, the only option left was to become Christians. Those who were considered as witches and traditional healers had to find a place to hide and the church was a good place to hide. The missionaries later noticed that many people were still carrying out their traditional beliefs and practices although they were

90. Byanafashe et al., "Teaching of History of Rwanda," 80.
91. Rutayisire, «Catholisme Rwandais,» 258.

baptized and had become church members.[92] For Andrew Walls, "it is the essence of the Gospel that God accepts us as we are, on the ground of Christ's work alone, not on the ground of what we have become or are trying to become."[93] Walls also points out that "In Christ God accepts us together with our group relations; with that cultural conditioning that makes us feel at home in one part of human society and less at home in another."[94] In the Rwandan case, people were not accepted as they were by missionaries. In Rwanda's mission history, missionaries gave the impression that people had to be transformed before God would accept them. At best, they worked hard to transform themselves into a given model of Christians as the way to being accepted by God. At worst, the church became merely a hiding place from persecution.

Rootless Christianity

When the genocide happened, which took the lives of over one million Tutsi, Rwanda was known as the most Christianized country in Africa. This is confirmed by Rutayisire in writing that:

> Le Rwanda a été qualifié par la presse missionnaire de « nation chrétienne », de « royaume chrétienne » après le geste symbolique posé par le Mwami Mutara III Rudahigwa de consacrer le Rwanda au Christ Roi en 1946, et même de « république chrétienne » après l'indépendance. Le génocide des Tutsi (avril-juillet 1994) a apporté un démenti à toutes ces constructions idéologiques qui cachaient mal leur limites et leurs aberration.[95]

> [Rwanda has been described by the missionary press as a "Christian nation" or "Christian kingdom" after the symbolic gesture by the Mwami Mutara III Rudahigwa of consecrating Rwanda to Christ the King in 1946, and even of "Christian republic" after the independence. The

---

92. Rutayisire, «Catholisme Rwandais,» 261.

93. Walls, *Missionary Movement in Christian History*, 7.

94. Walls, *Missionary Movement in Christian History*, 7.

95. Rutayisire, «Catholisme Rwandaise,» 257.

genocide of the Tutsi (April–July 1994) fostered a negative attitude to all these ideological constructions that barely concealed their limits and their aberrations.]

The genocide against Tutsis brought Rwanda's Christianity into scrutiny. In 1991, the statistics of Rwandans belonging to different religions showed the following: Catholics 62.6 percent of Rwanda's population, Protestants 18.8 percent, Adventists 8.4 percent, without religion 6.8 percent, and Muslims 1.2 percent.[96] Looking at these statistics, Rwanda was a Christian country. The question that arises is how the genocide was possible in such a Christian country. There may be many explanations, but Bishop Aloys Bigirumwami's confession before his death made it clear that he was sorry to have realized that Christianity was not rooted in Rwanda despite its many years of presence in the country.[97] Bishop Aloys Bigirumwami passed away in 1986, a few years before the genocide against Tutsi, and through his confession we notice that he was aware that Christianity was not rooted. It had not been planted in good soil because it was not spread by taking into consideration Rwandan primal religions. In seeing the primal religion as primitive, pagan, or traditional, it did not allow the missionaries and Rwandan elites, who took over the church after the missionaries, to value some good elements from Rwandan primal religion. As we noted earlier, the primal is important in mission and evangelization as it is the "basic, fundamental substratum."[98] This assertion implies that the primal religion should not be seen as primitive or traditional. This resounds in Bishop Aloys Bigirumwami's confession and warning to church leaders to take note. However, he remained the rare church leader in Rwanda who sought to raise awareness prior to the genocide against the Tutsi. After realizing the importance of primal religion, Bigirumwami did a great job of writing many books on Rwandan culture.

---

96. Commission Nationale de Recensement, *3ème Recensement générale de la population*, 60.

97. Bugurumwami, *Umuntu*, 99.

98. Bediako, "Primal Religion and Christian Faith," 12.

Christianity in Rwanda lacks the "fundamental substratum" due to the blank slate method used by missionaries in eradicating all traditions and practices related to Rwandan culture. Notwithstanding that, one good thing missionaries did was the introduction of formal education in Rwanda. Most of schools, elementaries, high schools, and later the universities were and still are church-based institutions. The missionary understanding of Rwandan primal religion prevailed, as the schools were following their curriculum with an agenda of civilizing Rwandans. Therefore, many Rwandan Christians had been living without their past. Andrew Walls affirms the past when he says that:

> It is our past which tells us who we are; without our past we are lost. The man with amnesia is lost, unsure of relationships, incapable of crucial decisions, precisely because all the time he has amnesia he is without his past. Only when his memory returns, when he is sure of his past, is he able to relate confidently to his wife, his parents, or know his place in society.[99]

Walls's argument may help us to answer the question of why the genocide was possible in a country considered to be Christian. People were lost due to the suppression of their past. Walls points out that "a man without a past is incapable of crucial decisions." Few Rwandans were able to say no to the genocide. The majority failed to stand up against the evil because they were "lost, or unsure of relationships." Our past is part of what makes us "who we are, what we have become," therefore ignoring it or trying to suppress it is tantamount to destroying our present.

Conclusion

In concluding this chapter, one thing is important to note: the majority of Western missionaries, whether Roman Catholic or Protestant, had a negative attitude toward Rwandan primal religions. This made them try to suppress primal religions in the

---

99. Walls, *Missionary Movement in Christian History*, 13.

process of Christianizing Rwanda. Thanks to Bishop Bigirumwami, today it is possible to know the pre-colonial Rwandan beliefs. The collection of Rwandan cultural, religious treasures and the writings of Bigirumwami on Rwandan culture are of rich value to scholars and all those involved in carrying on the mission of our Lord Jesus Christ. The following two chapters of this work focus on the life of Bigirumwami and the emergence of his concern for Rwandan primal religion, his advocacy for mother tongue use, and his Rwandan primal religion perception.

2

Bigirumwami and His Father's Unfulfilled Priesthood Calling

Introduction

IN THIS CHAPTER I discuss the early life of Aloys Bigirumwami, who was raised and educated by his father in a way that was unusual for the time. His father, being among the first Rwandans converted to Christianity, did not allow him to know much about his country's culture. The second point to be studied in this chapter is the emergence of his concern for Rwandan primal religion; how Bigirumwami, who was Westernized at a young age, came to the realization of the importance of primal religion for Christian faith.

Aloys Bigirumwami's Early Life

In his 1983 book *Umuntu*, while introducing himself to his readers, whom he assumed would be aged between thirty and seventy, Bigirumwami indicates that his father was one of the first Rwandans to convert to Christianity. The Roman Catholic missionaries arrived in Rwanda in 1900 and in 1903 on Christmas Day his father Rukamba Yozefu was baptized.[1] On Christmas Day in 1904 Bigirumwami was also baptized, two days after his birth. Bigirumwami indicates that he considered himself fortunate to

1. Bigirumwami, *Umuntu*, 7.

be among the first Rwandans baptized as infants.[2] This fact that he and his father were among the first Christians in Rwanda is very important in view of the later self-discovery and positive evaluation of the value of Rwandan pre-colonial culture, which was judged by others as evil at the time.

As already noted, Rukamba Yozefu, the father of Bigirumwami, was among the first Rwandans converted to Christianity through the Roman Catholic Church.[3] Bigirumwami indicates that his father was born approximately in 1884, during the reign of Rwabugiri.[4] Being the father of the one who became the first Roman Catholic Rwandan bishop, as well as one of the first Roman Catholic converts in Rwanda, Bishop Gasore later wrote a biography of Rukamba, entitled *Umukristu mu ba mbere bo mu Rwanda: Yozefu Rukamba*[5] [One Among the First Christians of Rwanda: Yozefu Rukamba]. In presenting the genealogy of Yozefu Rukamba, Gasore indicates that "Yozefu Rukamba is son of KARAKWE of RUCABASHISHA of RUSHENYI of MUHUTU of BAZIMYA of RUREGEYA of KWEZI of MUTUMINKA of NYAGISIZA. [Ubwoko][6] the clan is 'ABEGESERA.'"[7] Rukamba's mother was Kirebe, daughter of Zigaba.[8] Gasore further indicates that, according to the Zaza parish book, Rukamba was baptized on December 25, 1903, when he was nineteen years old, meaning that he was born in 1884.[9] Bigirumwami corroborates this, indicating

2. Bigirumwami, *Umuntu*, 7.

3. Bushayija, *Musenyeri Aloyizi Bigirumwami*, 12.

4. Bigirumwami, *Umuntu*, 101.

5. Gasore, *Umukristu mu ba mbere bo mu Rwanda*.

6. The word *ubwoko* had been used differently in Rwandan history. In precolonial Rwanda *ubwoko* referred to clan, but during the colonial period, when social classes were changed into ethnic groups, *ubwoko* was used in reference to ethnic group. In Rukamba's genealogy *ubwoko* is used in referring to "Abagesera clan." It is important to mention that it was possible for the three social groups (Abahutu, Abatwa, and Abatutsi) changed into ethnic groups to be part of the same clan.

7. Gasore, *Umukristu mu ba mbere bo mu Rwanda*, 9.

8. Gasore, *Umukristu mu ba mbere bo mu Rwanda*, 9.

9. Gasore, *Umukristu mu ba mbere bo mu Rwanda*, 9.

that when the white missionaries arrived in Rwanda in 1900, Ru-kamba was around sixteen to eighteen years old.[10] In October, the same year the priests started to build the Zaza parish, Rukamba started learning how to read and write by following the catechism lessons offered by the Roman Catholic priests.

Rukamba Becomes *Igisome*

The story of the first encounter of the missionaries with Rukamba is as follows: The priests, Bayiterema and Telebushi, went to Zaza from Buganza looking for a place where they could establish a Roman Catholic missionary station. After going around through-out Gisaka, they decided upon Ruhembe (Zaza).[11] As they were about to go back to Buganza, it started raining, ending a period of drought, and they ran to seek shelter in the nearby houses. The white fathers entered the house of Karakawe, the father of Rukam-ba. Given the fact that this was their first time seeing white men and seeing them come to their house, the Karakawe family mem-bers ran out from the house to hide themselves.[12] Gasore indicates that Karakawe was the only one who was not afraid and he of-fered them a seat. After the rain stopped, they left, telling him that they would return and take his son (Rukamba) so that he would start learning the catechism.[13] When Rukamba started learning the catechism, he was considered as *igisome*, meaning learned. For the local people, those who accepted learning the catechism or the teachings of the Roman Catholic missionaries were called *ibisome* (learned in plural) and they were considered as traitors, *inyangar-wanda*, meaning those who hate Rwandan learning, those who were abandoning the religion of their forefathers.[14] Being a quick learner, Rukamba was among those who were selected to continue

10. Bigirumwami, *Umuntu*, 101.

11. Gasore, *Umukristu mu ba mbere bo mu Rwanda*, 11.

12. Gasore, *Umukristu mu ba mbere bo mu Rwanda*, 11–12.

13. Gasore, *Umukristu mu ba mbere bo mu Rwanda*, 12.

14. Gasore, *Umukristu mu ba mbere bo mu Rwanda*, 11–14.

their studies at *Ihagiro* (Bukoba) seminary in Tanganyika, today's Tanzania. Karakwe was unhappy that his son had become *igisome*, and when he learned that his son was among those chosen for seminary he quickly organized a marriage for him. He provided dowry for Nyirabuskindoro and she became Rukamba's wife because he wished to prevent his son from becoming *igisome kitabyara*, meaning someone who is educated but who cannot give birth. This indicates that Karakwe was aware of Roman Catholic call for celibacy, especially for priests and nuns, and for Rwandans it was very important to give birth. Therefore Rukamba did not make it to the seminary due to his marriage. The first Rwandan to become a Roman Catholic priest was Gafuku, with whom he started learning the catechism.[15] Rukamba did not cease being a Roman Catholic; he was baptized together with fifty-four other Rwandans in 1903 by Priest Pouget (Terebushi), who baptized his son also in 1904.[16] Owing to the fact that they were the first Roman Catholic Church members, they had no spiritual parents and so the church was their spiritual parent.[17]

Rukamba struggled after his conversion to Christianity. His relationship with his father was poor; he told his son Bigirumwami that it was as if his father had banned him from the family.[18] When his father was sick, for example, Rukamba was asked to give one of his many hens to be used in *kuragura*, meaning divination, but he refused. This action was interpreted to mean he wanted the death of his father. It also aggravated his father's hostility towards him. When he died from an illness, Rukamba's Christian faith made him refuse to perform some Rwandan burial rites for his father. Bigirumwami describes the rite that Rukamba refused to perform:

> Tuvuye ku mva, bazanye amazi ku ruryo, n'ihundo ly'ishaka. Abali bageze ku mva bose baraza bakoza ino ly'ikirenge muli ya mazi, bakavuga: Uraze ukonje

---

15. Gasore, *Umukristu mu ba mbere bo mu Rwanda*, 14.

16. Gasore, *Umukristu mu ba mbere bo mu Rwanda*, 15.

17. Gasore, *Umukristu mu ba mbere bo mu Rwanda*, 11–14.

18. Bigirumwami, *Umuntu*, 103–4.

nk'amazi Bakaruma no ku ihundo, bakavuga ngo: Uzaze nk'amazi, usange ngukomereye nk'amakoma.[19]

[When we come from the tomb, they bring a half pot of water and an ear of sorghum. To all who are coming from the tomb, they all put their toe in the water saying: "May you come back cold like water," and they bite on the ear of sorghum saying: "Come back as water, and meet me strong as sorghum."]

Rukamba explains the ritual:

Ibyo byose babigiliraga guheza umuzimu wa data, ngo naramuka aje, azaze neza, asange bamukomereye nk'amakoma, azaze akonje nk'amazi, ntagire icyo abatwara! Bose barangije gukora ibyo, najye barabwira ngo ninkoze ino mu mazi, ngo nindume ku ihundo, ndanga, ndabahakanira. Barambwira ngo ubwo ntabikoze, birabe ibyanjye, ngo nzahuma, kandi nzapfa nabi.[20]

[They were doing all that so that when the ghost of my father comes back he would come peacefully, and meet them strong as sorghum, so that he would come as cold water and not harm them! When they finished doing all that, they asked me to put my toe in water, and bite on the ear of sorghum. I refused, I said no to them. They told me that because I did not do it it's my responsibility that I will be defiled and I will die a bad death.]

He was warned clearly that he would be alone when the *umuzimu*, meaning the ghost of his father, comes back with anger. Rukamba was caught between his new faith and his ancestors' culture. Two issues emerge from the narration of Rukamba and Karakwe: First, Rwandans were strongly holding on to their ancestral traditions to the extent of banning anyone who was going against it. Second, the first Rwandans converted to Christianity like Rukamba were caught between the church and their families. On the one hand they were asked by the church to abandon their ancestral traditions,

---

19. Bigirumwami, *Umuntu*, 104.

20. Bigirumwami, *Umuntu*, 104.

whereas on the other hand they were persecuted in their families to the point of being abandoned and losing their rights. As such Rukamba, the first son of his father, was not allowed to bury him; he attended the burial like an outsider. Becoming a Christian had made him a foreigner, even an enemy, of the family.

Rukamba Preparing Bigirumwami for Priesthood Calling

Rukamba's dream of going to Bukoba (Tanzania) for further studies to become a Roman Catholic priest was ended by the arranged marriage of his father. He could not at that point, at the beginning of the catechism, oppose his father's decision, for in his time parents, especially fathers, were deeply respected and he had no choice but to marry the girl chosen by his father and forget about becoming a priest.

There is a Rwandan proverb that says, "*Inyana ni iya mweru,*" literally "The heifer is for white," whose true meaning is "Like father like son." While Karakwe had arranged the marriage of Rukamba, the latter did everything possible to see his son fulfil his dream. He was not able to become a priest, but wanted his first son to become one. He therefore raised, educated, and took him to the seminary and finally he was happy to attend the ordination of his son as priest and later as the first Rwandan Roman Catholic bishop. How did Rukamba prepare Bigirumwami for priesthood? Two factors may help us to answer the question.

A Military Style of Education

Bigirumwami was not only one of the first Rwandan children to receive baptism, but among the first Rwandan children to receive a formal education also. His father was *igisome*, meaning that he could read and write. Bigrumwami indicates that:

> Ntangira kumenya ubwenge nasanze Data baramunter-
> ereje, ngo ntatume ngira uko nigira. Iyo atangeza vuba
> mu Semiraniri, sinzi ko mba naramukize. Dore ubwira

yagize bwo kumburabuza, ni bwo bwangejeje ku musozi mutagatifu, kuri Altari ya Mungu, mba umusaserdoti n'umupiskop, . . . Sinzi aho data yakuye umuco w'abasoda baburabuzwa igihe cyose, bagahanirwa ikibaye cyose. Na n'ubu sindibagirwa inkeke nilirwagaho. Data niwe wanyigishije gusoma no kwandika vuba vuba, mbimenya vuba, anjyana vuba mu Seminari. Niwe wambujije kumenya andi mayira, keretse inzira yo kuva imuhira no mu Misiyoni, no kuva mu Misiyoni ntaha imuhira.[21]

[When I started gaining knowledge, it seems that there was an arranged conspiracy between my father and someone telling him not allowing me to do what I want to do. If he had not been able to take me quickly to the seminary, I don't know if I would have survived him. His insistence on not giving me peace is what took me to the holy mountain, to the altar of God; I became a priest and a bishop. I don't know where my father got the military culture from. The soldiers are the ones disturbed every time, and punished for everything that happens. Even today I cannot forget the anxiety, worry that my father put me through every day. My father was the one to teach me reading and writing quickly, and I learnt very fast; he took me to the seminary. He was the one who made it impossible for me to know what other children of my age were doing. I had only one way, that of going to the mission station and back home.]

Rukamaba, who had seen his dream of becoming a priest ended by his father, did not give his son the room to make a choice. He knew that it had been the community's understanding that influenced his father's decision to arrange a quick marriage for him, and so in order to protect his son he gave him a military style of education. But apart from that his father loved him and wanted him to become a priest. He further indicates that:

Bwaracyaga kare kare, data akambyutsa, akanyuhagira vuba, akanyambika, akanshyira imbere ye tukajya mu misa, yarangira nkajya mu ishuli, nava mu ishuli ngataha

21. Gasore, *Umukristu mu ba mbere bo mu Rwanda*, 4.

vuba, kuko yigeze kunkubitira ko natinze mu nzira . . .
Uwantereje data ngo yilirwe antera sentili, yali yaramub-
wiye ngo nibumara kwira antoneshe, ambyinishe,
ankikire, anyweshe amata, ansomye inzoga, angeze ku
buliri, anyibagize akazi k'umunsi.[22]

[Next day, early in the morning, my father would wake
me up, wash me quickly, and put me ahead of him to go
to mass. At the end of mass I had to go to school; after
class I had to go home quickly, because one day he beat
me because I took a long time to reach home . . . The
one who had told my father to beat me with a belt had
told him when the evening comes to spoil me, make me
dance, carry me on his lap, make me drink milk and beer
during the evening, put me to bed, and make me forget
all that I had done the whole day.]

In Rukamba's time, for a man to wash his son, clothe him,
and put him to bed was seen as *kuba inganzwa,* meaning to be a
man dominated by his wife, because the society was patriarchal.
But Rukamba knew what he was doing and why he was being
strict and concerned about his son's education. He was ready to
do anything for his son, so wanting him to be focused to the
point of beating him just because he had looked back during
mass.[23] But as Bigirumwami mentioned above, all that his father
did played a remarkable role in his ordination as Roman Catholic
priest, bishop, and servant of God.

Rukamba's Letter to Bigirumwami

Bigirumwami spent nine years in the seminary without visiting
his parents, as it was not allowed in his time. He indicates that his
father visited him twice during the nine years. In a biography on
Bigirumwami, Antoni Bushayisha writes about a copy of Rukamba's

---

22. Gasore, *Umukristu mu ba mbere bo mu Rwanda,* 4–5.
23. Gasore, *Umukristu mu ba mbere bo mu Rwanda,* 5.

letter sent to Bigirumwami when he was about to enter in the major seminary in 1921.[24] In the letter his father made it clear:

> Mwana wajye, tega amatwi: ngiye kukubwira amagambo y'amashirakinyoma. Waravutse ndakurera, hanyuma Imana ikwereka inzira igushakamo...Nari naguhawe n'Imana, none nanjye nguhaye Imana.[25]

> [My child, listen to me: I want to tell you without lying to you. You were born, and I raised you; after that God took you on the way he wants you on . . . I was given you by God, and I'm also giving you to God.]

Rukamba in his letter clearly indicates that he is the one who offered his son to God, though he knew that God was the one who chose his son first. He was concerned about his son's calling and asked him to be careful and commit to the work of God as the path that he was on was difficult, but he should trust God.[26]

Even from afar, Rukamba kept a close eye on the education of his son, advising him and encouraging him to focus on the work of serving God. As Bigirumwami pointed it out, *"hashize imyaka 60, ubu ni ho numva akamaro k'akarasisi kandeze, ni ho nibuka ineza yose data yangiliye"*[27] [it is after sixty years that I understand now the importance of the military parade that educated me; it is now that I remember the goodness of my father towards me]. Thanks to his education and discipline by Bigirumwami's father, Rwanda had its first Rwandan Roman Catholic bishop, as well as one of the theologians who started the process of inculturation or contextualization of Christianity in Rwanda.

Aloys Bigirumwami was blessed to be one of the first children to have Christian parents; therefore he was baptised as a baby and received formal education that enabled him to be accepted into the seminary school. Due to his father's education and discipline, he was not able to live like normal children of his time, as he was

24. Bushayija, *Musenyeri Aloyizi Bigirumwami*, IV Annexe, 93.

25. Bushayija, *Musenyeri Aloyizi Bigirumwami*, IV Annexe, 93.

26. Bushayija, *Musenyeri Aloyizi Bigirumwami*, IV Annexe, 93.

27. Gasore, *Umukristu mu ba mbere bo mu Rwanda*, 5.

given a military-style education by his father. Rukamba, who had not been allowed to enter seminary and become a priest, did everything possible to see his son achieve that goal. As his father, Karakwe, had arranged marriage for him, Rukamba also played a remarkable role in preparing Bigirumwami for seminary.

The Seminary Years

Bigirumwami was taken to Kabgayi minor seminary by his father when he was ten years old and he spent nine years without seeing his mother, brothers, and sisters.[28] Schools were one of the instruments used by Western missionaries in the process of Westernizing Rwandans. Talking about his experience, Bigirumwami indicates that:

> Durant 15 ans de formation au petit et au grand séminaire, j'ai épousé plutôt la mentalité, les expressions et les gestes des mes professeurs français, belges, hollandais, italiens. « Dis-moi qui-tu hantes, je te dirai qui tu es ». « Uburere buruta ubuvuke" disons-nous; c'est à dire : l'éducation et la formation sont plus importantes pour la personnalité que la reproduction.[29]

> [During fifteen years of formation at the minor and the major seminary, I adopted rather the mentality, the expressions, and the gestures of my French, Belgian, Dutch, and Italian teachers. "Tell me who you haunt; I'll tell you who you are." "Uburere buruta ubuvuke," we say; that education and training are more important to the personality than just giving birth to a child.]

Due to the fact that seminarians were not allowed to go back home, they adopted the lifestyle of their teachers. This made them foreigners in their own country, even to the level of forgetting their parents. Bigirumwami indicates that he was very happy to read Gasore's book on his father due to the fact that he had not

---

28. Bigirumwami, *Umuntu*, 9.
29. Bigirumami, Rites, «Proverbes et Fables,» 3.

known his parents, brothers, and sisters very well.[30] Apart from talking about how the many years of absence made him forget his mother's face, as well as his brothers and sisters, Bigirumwami explained why they were not allowed to go home during vacation. They were told that their homes were far from school, but there were other reasons which they did not mention. Not all students came from far away; so as Bigirumwami indicates there may have been other reasons.[31] In his book *Umuntu*, Bigirumwami elaborates further: "*Mfite imyaka cumi, data yanjyanye I Kabgayi mu seminari. Bamfungira mu rugo rwa seminari ntoya imyaka 7 no mu seminari nkuru imyaka 8, kuko batubuzaga kugera iwacu.*"[32] [When I was ten years old, my father took me to Kabgayi to the seminary. I was locked in the enclosure of minor seminary for seven years and in the enclosure of major seminary for eight years, because they didn't want us to go back to our homes.] The word *Bamfungira* comes from the verb *Gufunga*, meaning to lock, to tie up, which has strong meaning because from it comes *imfungwa*, meaning prisoner. In other words, Bigirumwami is saying that he was a prisoner for seven years in minor seminary and eight years in major seminary. The root of the word *Bamfungira* is *Ba*, meaning they, representing the school leadership. The seminary was under the Roman Catholic missionaries, who at the time were all from Europe. Therefore, for Bigirumwami they were the ones responsible for preventing students from visiting their family during holidays. Bigirumwami further indicates that "*Kwihunza ababyeyi n'abavandimwe, byitwaga gutandukana n'ab'isi n'iby'isi*"[33] [To flee from parents and siblings was called separating yourself from worldly people and worldly things]. In the period that seminarians were far from their parents, they were also estranged from who they were, because our past is part of who we are. It was in families that Rwandans were taught about their past and culture.

30. Gasore, *Umukristu mu ba mbere bo mu Rwanda*, 3.

31. Gasore, *Umukristu mu ba mbere bo mu Rwanda*, 3.

32. Bigirumwami, *Umuntu*, 98.

33. Bigirumwami, *Umuntu*, 11.

Discussing why he wanted to learn about his country's culture Bigirumwami, indicates that:

> Je n'ai pratiquement pas vécu dans ma famille à l'âge ou j'aurais pu jouir et profiter des bonnes causeries durant la veillée: des contes, des chants et de toute la sagesse traditionnelle de notre pays. Ce la m'a laissé un regret et une saine curiosité qui m'a poussé a la recherche des coutumes, des dictons, proverbes, fables, devinettes : de toute la richesse de la culture Rwandaise dont je n'ai pas eu connaissance dans mon jeune âge.[34]

> [I practically did not live with my family at the age where I could enjoy good conversations during the evening gathering of: tales, songs, and all the traditional wisdom of our country. This has left me with regret and a healthy curiosity that drove me in search of customs, sayings, proverbs, fables, riddles: all the wealth of Rwandan culture that I did not know in my youth.]

Seminarians were taken at a young age, when they were supposed to be learning their culture through evening gathering called *Igitaramo*, where many activities were held such as hearing poems, singing, dancing, etc. They were trained in seminaries to see their parents and siblings as worldly people from whom they should separate themselves. Living with their parents and siblings was tantamount to going back to worldly people. Bigirumwami clearly indicates that after seminary studies he had to ask the church members of his parish to teach him through writing down everything that they knew about Rwandan culture.[35] Clearly, in the seminary he learned nothing about Rwandan culture.

Clergy Years

After completing his seminary studies and ordination as priest in 1929, Bigirumwami was appointed to the Muramba parish in 1930.

---

34. Bigirumwami, «mes frères dans le Sacerdoce.»
35. Bigirumwami, *Umuntu*, 10.

According to Antoni Bushayija Bugabo, on May 26, 1929, when Aloys Bigirumwami was ordained as a Roman Catholic priest he became the tenth Rwandan priest.[36] From 1931 to 1932, Bigirumwami was sent to Kigali to *Umulyango mutagatifu*, meaning the Holy Family Parish. From 1933 to 1951 he served in the Muramba parish, located at the time in Satinskyi (Satinsyi) District, Gisenyi Prefecture, where he served for eighteen years. Bigirumwami arrived in the Muramba parish in 1933, when many Rwandans were converting to Christianity. He trained catechists and neophytes who were also to help in teaching the parish members. To help Christians he also started a literacy program to help them to be able to read and write. He had to attend to many new believers, by teaching them and visiting them in their homes. His pastoral work of attending to the church members by visiting them, being closer to his parish members, led his superiors to nominate him as member of Vicariate Council.[37] His pastoral ministry was carried out alongside his work of collecting pre-colonial Rwandan traditions. In 1951 the Nyundo parish was celebrating fifty years of existence when Bigirumwami was sent to be the head priest of the parish. To be the one chosen to take over the Nyundo parish after the death of priest A. Pages, who has been in the parish for twenty years, was a great sign that Bigirumwami was being prepared for high office.[38], Bigirumwami was the Bishop of the Nyundo diocese from1952 until 1974, when he wrote to the pope asking permission to resign before his retirement age.

Creation of Nyundo Vicariate and Appointment of Bigirumwami as Bishop

After celebrating the jubilee of evangelization in Rwanda, Bishop Déprimoz, who was heading up the Roman Catholic Church in

36. Bushayija, *Musenyeri Aloyizi Bigirumwami*, 19.

37. Editions du Secrétariat général de la CEPR, *Hommage a Mgr Aloys Bigirumwami*, 13.

38. Bushayija, *Musenyeri Aloys Bigirumwami*, 20.

Rwanda, proposed the division of the Rwandan vicariate[39] into two. Bushayija quotes Bishop Déprimoz saying that:

> Turebye aho u Rwanda rugeze n'iterambere ryarwo, ndemeza ntashidikanya ko igihe kigeze ngo abapadiri b'Abanyarwanda (clergé indigène) bagire uruhare mu miyoborere ya Kiliziya Gatorika yo mu gihugu cyabo.[40]

> [Looking at where Rwanda is today and at its development, I confirm without hesitation that it's time for Rwandan priests (indigenous clergy) to play a role in leading the Catholic Church of their own country.

The Roman Catholic Church in Rwanda belongs to Rwandans and it was time for Rwandan priests to be in leadership of the church. Yet even though Bishop Déprimoz approved "indigenous clergy" heading up the church in theory, he still had doubts that a Rwandan priest could take up that responsibly and carry it out effectively. He therefore proposed that the second vicariate be created and should be located in a rural area remote from many Western missionaries and visitors. The southern part of Rwanda, near Burundi, where the Belgian colonial administration was based, was then well developed and not considered suitable for the new Rwandan bishop. Déprimoz first proposed the northern part of Rwanda, which was at the time still rural.[41] Bushayija indicates that Alexis Kagame, a Rwandan priest who came to know about the new

39. «Au plan de l'administration pastorale, le Rwanda était alors régi par le statut canonique de vicariat apostolique. On entend par la 'une portion déterminée du peuple de Dieu qui, a cause des circonstances particulières, n'est pas encore constituée en diocèse, et dont la charge pastorale est confiée a un Vicaire Apostolique . . . qui la gouverne au nom du Pontife Suprême' (Code de droit canonique, Can371§1).» Editions du Secrétariat général de la CEPR, *Hommage a Mgr Aloys Bigirumwami*, 56. [At the level of pastoral administration, Rwanda was then governed by the canonical status of apostolic vicariate. We mean by that 'a determined portion of the people of God who, because of the particular circumstances, is not yet constituted in the diocese, and whose pastoral charge is entrusted to an Apostolic Vicar . . . who governs in the name of the Pontiff Supreme' (Code of Canon Law, Can371§1).]

40. Bushayija, *Musenyeri Aloys Bigirumwami*, 22.

41. Bushayija, *Musenyeri Aloys Bigirumwami*, 22–23.

vicariate, expressed his displeasure. For him it was a kind of trap, revealing a belief that local priests were not capable of heading the church. For Priest Kagame, the vicariate was being proposed for a rural area where it would be difficult for an "indigenous priest" to carry out his ministry.[42] Yet the new vicariate was finally created in the rural area of the northwest part of Rwanda:

> ... nous détachons du vicariat du Ruanda toute la région qui s'étend a l'ouest des lacs Bulera et Ruhondo, et au nord des fleuves dits Mukungwa, Nyabarongo, Mbiru-rume et Kilimbi et dans laquelle sont situées les stations missionnaires de Nyundo, Muramba, Rambura, Nyange, Birambo et Muhororo. Toute cette région nous l'érigeons et la constituons en nouveau vicariat apostolique qui sera appelé « de Nyundo.»[43]

> [... we are detaching from the vicariate of Rwanda all the area extending west of Bulera and Ruhondo lakes, and north of the so-called Mukungwa, Nyabarongo rivers, Mbirurume and Kilimbi, where the missionary stations of Nyundo, Muramba, Rambura, Nyange, Birambo, and Muhororo are located. This entire region we erect and make it a new apostolic vicariate to be called "Nyundo."]

The decree further indicates that the new vicariate was to be given to "indigenous priests," who would know the characters and morals of their citizens.[44] In his letter to Rome recommending three Rwandan priests (Aloys Bigirumwami, Yozefu Sibomana, and Yohani Bizimana) for one of them to be chosen as the bishop of the new vicariate, Bishop Déprimoz did not conceal his preference for Bigirumwami. "*Ubundi uko mbabona kandi mbishyize n'imbere y'Imana, nsanga umwe muri bo ariwe urushije abo bandi bombi kuba yayoborana ubuhanga n'ubushobozi. Akaba*

---

42. Bushayija, *Musenyeri Aloys Bigirumwami*, 23.

43. Editions du Secrétariat général de la CEPR, *Hommage a Mgr Aloys Bigirumwami*, 15.

44. Editions du Secrétariat général de la CEPR, *Hommage a Mgr Aloys Bigirumwami*, 15.

ari padiri Aloys Bigirumwami."[45] [In fact, the way I see them, and I put it before God, I realize one of them is ahead of the two others, to be able to lead with intelligence and capacity. It is Priest Aloys Bigirumwami.] His recommendation was taken into consideration and Bigirumwami was the one selected to be the bishop of the new vicariate. The new vicariate was located in the mountainous region, where Christianity was not as widespread as in the southern part. The region was poor in terms of human resources and materials to use for the ministry.[46] Some Rwandan priests went to Bigirumwami asking him to refuse the new vicariate and ask for the Astrid (Butare) in the southern part of Rwanda. But Bigirumwami responded to them, "*Mpawe umushike kandi nzawuhinga*"[47] [I'm given a difficult land to cultivate; I will cultivate it]. Though other Rwandan priests were not happy and fearful for his failure, for Bigirumwami, it was a challenge that he was ready to take up and demonstrate that African priests were capable of taking over in leading the church.

On July 1, 1952, Bigirumwami was ordained as bishop,[48] thus becoming the first "indigenous clergy" to be appointed bishop in the Belgian colonies of Africa.[49] The king of Rwanda, colonial Belgian authorities, Roman Catholic missionaries from Rwanda and Burundi, and more than twenty-five thousand persons attended his ordination. The new bishop (Bigirumwami) chose a motto from the Epistle of Paul to the Romans, chapter 13:12: "*Induamur arma luci*"[50] [Let's put on the weapons of light]. The period for Rwandan clergy to be behind in church leadership was over and it was their time to put on the armor of light and lead the church

45. Bushayija, *Musenyeri Aloys Bigirumwami*, 24–25.

46. Editions du Secrétariat général de la CEPR, *Hommage a Mgr Aloys Bigirumwami*, 16–17.

47. Bushayija, *Musenyeri Aloys Bigirumwami*, 24.

48. Editions du Secrétariat général de la CEPR, *Hommage a Mgr Aloys Bigirumwami*, 20.

49. Editions du Secrétariat général de la CEPR, *Hommage a Mgr Aloys Bigirumwami*, 13.

50. Editions du Secrétariat général de la CEPR, *Hommage a Mgr Aloys Bigirumwami*, 20.

of their country. One of Bigirumwami's first challenges was to look for collaborators to work within the new vicariate. Bigirumwami refused to take missionaries who were already serving in Rwanda or in other African countries. Bigirumwami went looking for European seminarians who would accept to come and serve full-time in the Diocese of Nyundo. They were to continue their theological studies at the Major Nyakibanda Seminary and serve in the Nyundo diocese after their ordination as priests, like their Rwandan colleagues.[51] Bigirumwami wanted young missionaries willing to learn first and then serve after. He knew the importance of missionaries learning in the country where they had to serve. His experience indicates how much he was for inculturation of the gospel in Rwanda.

The Conférence Episcopale du Rwanda (CEPR) indicates that when Bigirumwami was given Nyundo in 1952 only four congregations were present in some parishes. CEPR points out Bigirumwami's achievements over twenty years:

> Ainsi en 20 ans, fonda-t- il 13 paroisses et plusieurs écoles primaires. Le nombre d'écoliers grandit; il passa de 3.981 écoliers dans 218 classes en 1952 à 70.000 écoliers dans 1.400 classes en 1972. Il n'y avait aucune école secondaire dans le diocèse en 1952. En 1973 il y aura sept écoles pour fille et 7 pour garçons. Le grand Séminaire Saint Joseph sera fondé en Octobre 1963.[52]

> [Thus in 20 years, he founded 13 parishes and several primary schools. The number of school children increased; it passed from 3.981 school children in 218 classes in 1952 to 70,000 school children in 1,400 classes in 1972. There was no secondary school in the diocese in 1952. In 1973 there were seven schools for girls and seven for boys. The major Saint Joseph Seminary was founded in October 1963.]

51. Editions du Secrétariat général de la CEPR, *Hommage a Mgr Aloys Bigirumwami*, 21.

52. Editions du Secrétariat général de la CEPR, *Hommage a Mgr Aloys Bigirumwami*, 22.

Bishop Déprimoz and other Roman Catholic priests had been afraid concerning the capacity of indigenous clergy to lead a vicariate and created a rural vicariate where they could observe the leadership of new local bishop. Bigirumwami did much to carry on the development of the Nyundo diocese in terms of church expansion and changing members' lives. He promoted social action to improve the lives of people in the diocese by bringing in organizations from Europe to serve, especially from Liège Diocese in Belgium, with which Bigirumwami had signed a partnership. This explains why his Rwandan colleagues in their writings kept highlighting Bigirumwami's achievements by comparing the number of schools and parishes under his leadership with those existing prior to his assuming the leadership role as bishop.

Useful Retreat for Research

After his resignation as bishop of the Nyundo diocese, Bigirumwami went to the Kivumu parish, where he spent five years, and in 1979 he went in the retreat house at Kigufi near Lake Kivu.[53] Bigirumwami, who had built up an enormous collection on Rwandan traditions from the whole country, used his retreat period to continue writing and publishing books on Rwandan culture. Muzungu indicates that:

> Après sa démission de sa charge pastorale d'Evêque de Nyundo, Mgr BIGIRUMWAMI n'est pas allé dans sa solitude de Kivumu et de Kigufi pour prendre un repos mérité. Il a utilisé ce temps matériel pour reprendre la masse des informations qu'il venait de réunir et de publier. Il s'est mis à les examiner patiemment, à les comprendre et à les interpréter à la lumière de sa foi chrétienne pour cueillir le fruit qu'elles contenaient.[54]

> [After his resignation from his pastoral office as Bishop of Nyundo, Bishop BIGIRUMWAMI did not go to the

53. Bigirumwami, *Umuntu*, 7.
54. Muzungu, «Centenaire Du Clerge Rwandais,» 44.

loneliness of Kivumu and Kigufi to take a well-deserved rest. He used this time to assimilate the mass of information he had just gathered and published. He began to examine them patiently, to understand them and to interpret them in the light of his Christian faith to pick the fruit they contained.]

Bigirumwami's first books were collections of material he had gathered. After his resignation he started analyzing the information that he had gathered, both published and not yet published. It is during this period that he wrote his book *Umuntu*, which is like an encyclopedia of his writings. CEPR issued some of his major publications.[55]

---

55. The following are Bigirumwami's publications issued by CEPR:

1. *Imihango n'imigenzo n'imiziririzo mu Rwanda* [Rites, Customs, and Taboos in Rwanda] (Nyundo, 1964),

2. *Imihango yo kuraguza, Guterekera, Kubandwa Nyabingi* [Divination Practices, Ancestral Spirits Worship, Initiatory Worship of Lyagombe, and That of Nyabingi] (Nyundo, 1968). The two volumes were republished as one book, *Imihango n'imigenzo n'imiziririzo mu Rwanda* (Nyundo, 2004).

3. *Imigani Migufi, Inshamarenga, Ibisakuzo* [Proverbs, Idiomatic Phrases, and Riddles] (Nyundo, 1967).

4. *Imigani Miremire* [Tales or Fables] (Nyundo, 1971).

5. *Ibitekerezo, Indirimbo n'imbyino, Ibihozo n'inanga, Ibyivugo, Amazina y'inka n'amahamba, Ibiganiro* [Historical Stories and Legends, Folk Songs and Dances, Lullabies, War Poetry, Pastoral Poetry, Jokes] (Nyundo, 1972).

6. "Rites, Proverbes, et Fables au Rwanda," in *Culture traditionnelle et Christianisme* (Nyundo, 1969).

7. «Présentation et commentaire des cinq volumes écrits par Mgr Bigirumwami,» in *Foi et Culture* 38 (January–March 1972) 1–74.

8. «La religion traditionnelle au Rwanda,» in *Aspects de la culture rwandaise*, ed. Centre de Bibliographie rwandaise de UNR Butare (1972), 60–75.

9. *Imana y'abantu, Abantu b'Imana* [God of People, People of God] (Nyundo, 1976).

10. *Umuntu, Barabwira, Baribwira, Barabwirwa, baterariyo* [Human

The first seminaries in Rwanda were formed for one purpose: to train good pastors who would spread the gospel of Jesus Christ to their fellow Rwandans. When many Roman Catholic clergy came together to write a book in the memory of Bigirumwami, they were amazed by his intellectual capacity. They took note of the fact that Bigirumwami was not only known as a good bishop, but a researcher and writer[56] as well. They further indicated how noteworthy that was:

> . . . a l'époque de sa jeunesse, les programmes des études au petit comme au grand Séminaire n'étaient pas telle-ment aussi riches, aussi ouvert à la science qu'aujourd'hui. Ce qui alors était considéré comme prioritaire pour la formation des futurs prêtres indigènes au Rwanda, ce n'était pas d'en faire des intellectuels, mais plutôt de bons pasteurs d'âmes. Jean Marie Vianney, le saint Cure d'Ars, était généralement cité en exemple dans ce sens.[57]

> [. . . at the time of his youth, the programs of study at the minor as well as at the major seminary were not so rich and as open to science as they are today. What was then considered as a priority for the training of future indigenous priests in Rwanda was not enough to make them intellectuals, but rather good pastors of souls. Jean Marie Vianney, the saint Cure d'Ars, was generally cited as an example in this sense.]

Bigirumwami went beyond being just a priest by engaging in research in order to help those who would come after him not to have to struggle as he did. Seeing what he had achieved, Bigi-rumwami did not depart from his calling on an intellectual quest. Rather, he carried out his ministry alongside intellectual work. It went hand in hand with his main role of heading the church.

. . .]. The title is difficult to translate into other languages, but it's about three types of humans. (Nyundo, 1983). In Editions du Secrétariat général de la CEPR, *Hommage a Mgr Aloys Bigirumwami*, 95–97.

56. Editions du Secrétariat général de la CEPR, *Hommage a Mgr Aloys Bigirumwami*, 75.

57. Editions du Secrétariat général de la CEPR, *Hommage a Mgr Aloys Bigirumwami*, 75.

Emergence of Bigirumwami's Concern
for Rwandan Primal Religion

Bigirumwami indicates that when he was serving at Parish Umury-ango Mutagatifu ("Holy Family") Kigali, he faced a problem of comprehending what people were saying:

> Mu wa 1931–1932, ndi I Kigali, muli paruwasi y'Umul-yango Mutagatifu, nararebaga nkabona abantu bansha mu maso, nategaga amatwi, ngasanga ntumva; navuga (ngira Imana bakantinyuka), bati: Wavukiye he? Ugize ngo iki? Ni bwo nibwiye nti: Nzamenya abantu nte? Ibya-bo nzabyumva nte? Imihango n'Imizilirizo bajya bavuga ni bite? Abazimu batera bate? Baraguza bate? Baterekera bate? Babandwa bate?[58]

> [In 1931–1932, at Parish Umulyango Mutagatifu of Ki-gali, I use to see people passing by; I used to hear what they were saying, but I realized that I was not under-standing what they were saying. I can say that I was lucky (some were not afraid of me) and asked: Where were you born? What are you saying? Then I told myself: How will I know people? How will I hear about their ways? What about the traditions, usages, and taboos that they talk about? How the ghosts attack people? How did they carry out divination? How did they appease or please the spirits of the dead? How was Kubandwa carried out?]

Bigirumwami's dilemma shows that he was like a foreigner in his own country. Realizing that he was not able to effectively communicate the gospel to his church members as he should, Bigirumwami asked them to help him to get to know his cul-ture, especially the pre-colonial Rwandan religion. From 1932 to 1967 he supplied paper to many people for the purpose of writ-ing down everything that they knew about proverbs, traditions, stories, dances, and songs. He indicates that he did this across the whole country, with the result that he gathered a collection from

---

58. Bigirumwami, *Umuntu*, 10.

different parts of Rwanda.[59] In the beginning his main purpose was not to understand pre-colonial Rwandan primal religion as something good on which to build the Christian faith, but to be able to condemn it well.

> Primitivement, mes recherchés sur la connaissance des traditions dites payennes avaient pout but le rejet et la condamnation pures et simples des us et coutumes : « Itegeko lya mbere litubuza kuraguza no guterekera no kubandwa n'indi mihango yose idakwiye. Comme dit le text de notre catechisme. . . [60]

> [Originally, my research on the knowledge of the so-called pagan traditions had for its goal the pure and simple rejection and condemnation of the customs: *"Itegeko lya mbere litubuza kuraguza no guterekera no kubandwa n'indi mihango yose idakwiye."* "The first law forbids us to engage in divination, to appease or please the ghosts, Kubandwa and other unacceptable rites," as the text of our catechism says . . .]

Bigirumwami further indicates that he spent thirty years, including eighteen at the Muramba parish, persecuting Rwandan traditions. It was only gradually that Bigirumwami changed his perception toward Rwandan primal religion. He indicates that "Ma conversion lente et difficile de croire que les payens adorent Dieu et que « Dieu aime les payens » surgit à la suite de l'examen attentif, comme 'a la loupe' ou 'au microscope' des us et coutumes traditionnels"[61] [My slow and difficult conversion to believe that the pagans adore God and that "God loves the pagans" arises as a result of careful examination, such as "under the microscope" of traditional habits and customs]. Bigirumwami was not only influenced by his close study of Rwandan primal religion, for he also indicated that "ma conversion se poursuivit dans la méditation de Vatican II, des lettres du Pape Paul VI et de quelques auteurs missiologues" [My conversion continued through reflection on

---

59. Bigirumwami, *Umuntu*, 10.

60. Bigirumwami, «Rites, Proverbes et Fables,» 3.

61. Bigirumwami, «Rites, Proverbes et Fables,» 3.

Vatican II, letters from Pope Paul VI and some missiologist writers]. In the preamble of Vatican II's "Declaration on the Relations of the Church of God with Non-Christian Religions," it is stated:

> A notre époque où le genre humain devient de jour en jour plus étroitement uni et où les relations entre les divers peuples augmentent, l'Eglise examine plus attentivement quelle est son attitude à l'égard des religions non chrétiennes. Dans sa mission de promouvoir l'unité et la charité entre les hommes, et même entre les peuples, elle examine ici d'abord ce que les hommes ont en commun et qui les pousse à vivre ensembles leur destinée.[62]

> [In our time, when the human race is becoming more and more closely united day by day, and relations among the various peoples are increasing, the church is more attentive to her attitude towards non-Christian religions. In her mission to promote unity and charity between people, and even between peoples, she first examines what men have in common and which pushes them to live out their destiny.]

Like Vatican II, Bigirumwami's attitude towards non-Christian religion shifted from rejection and condemnation to an appreciation of the positive elements from primal religion and a belief that it is possible to build on them in spreading the gospel. What makes Bigirumwami's testimony about his progressive conversion noteworthy is the fact that it was given first to clergy and lay Roman Catholics who attended the first ever conference on "Traditional Culture and Christianity" organized by the Nyundo diocese in 1969.[63] Bigirumwami knew that some of his colleagues were not in favor of the idea of considering primal religion as important for the gospel.[64] He wanted them to take time like him to read and research on Rwandan culture in order to realize its importance. In one of the letters of Pope Paul VI to Africa, "Message à l'Afrique," he indicates that

---

62. Henry, ed., *Vatican II*, 25.

63. Bigirumwami, «Rites, Proverbes et Fables,» 5–6.

64. Bigirumwami, «Rites, Proverbes et Fables,» 12.

there is moral and religious value in ancient African culture.[65] His message was well captured by Bigirumwami, who started pointing out those moral and religious values in the Rwandan context in the paper "Rites, Proverbes et Fables au Rwanda," which he presented during the sacerdotal conference in 1969.[66]

Bigirumwami had started out convinced that if a Rwandan said he/she was a Christian but had not adopted a European mentality, he/she was not yet a Christian. He later came to the point of realizing that one can become a Christian without changing one's Rwandan mentality.[67]

> Aujourd'hui, je ne voudrais plus être qu'un chrétien africain, rwandais et non un chrétien européanisé, belge ou français ou espagnol. Mon souhait est de voir mes compatriotes convertis à l'Evangile sans devoirs se renier et sans renoncer a leurs bonnes habitudes traditionnelles.[68]

> [Today, I would like to be an African, Rwandan and not a Europeanized, Belgian or French or Spanish Christian. My wish is to see my compatriots converted to the gospel without having to deny themselves and without giving up their traditional good habits.]

Bigirumwami's main objective thus became one of preserving the religious, moral, familial, social, and political traditions of Rwanda.[69] He therefore continued collecting Rwandan traditions across the country and writing books on Rwandan culture for two main reasons: First, African traditions and Rwandan in particular were of immense value and should be appreciated and recognized. Second, the mother tongue is to be used in spreading the gospel, and primal religions are to be studied and built on to promote a Rwandan Christian faith.

---

65. Bigirumwami, «Rites, Proverbes et Fables,» 4.

66. Bigirumwami, «Rites, Proverbes et Fables,» 5–6.

67. Bigirumwami, «Rites, Proverbes et Fables,» 3.

68. Bigirumwami, «Rites, Proverbes et Fables,» 3.

69. Bigirumwami, «Rites, Proverbes et Fables,» 3.

Conclusion

Bigirumwami had been unable to learn Rwandan culture due to the fact that he was taken to seminary at an early age, and he became a foreigner in his own country. When he started serving as a priest he was unable to communicate the gospel effectively due to the fact that he was a Western-trained evangelist, a foreigner to Rwandans who were still holding on to their cultural heritage. Therefore, he felt the need to study Rwandan primal religion in order to be able to reject and condemn it well. In the process, he came to realize that what was considered as evil had some good elements. Close and careful study of the traditions, the influence of Vatican II, letters of Pope Paul VI, and some works of missiology helped him to give much attention to Rwandan primal religion. His long journey of collecting and writing about Rwandan culture continued till his death on June 3, 1986.[70]

---

70. Muzungu, "Bishop Aloys Bigirumwami," 79.

3

Mother Tongue and Rwandan Primal Religion in Bigurumwami's Written Works

Introduction

IN HIS TWO FINAL books, *Imana y'Abantu*[1] and *Umuntu*,[2] Bigirumwami presented his deep meditation on the mystery of man and God. In studying Rwandan traditions, rites, customs, and taboos, he came to the understanding that Rwandans knew God before the arrival of colonizers and Western missionaries. Kinyarwanda played a major role in Bigirumwami's study of pre-colonial traditions to the extent that he chose to write his books in Kinyarwanda. In this chapter I shall focus firstly on Bigirumwami and mother tongue usage and later I will discuss his views of Rwandan primal religion.

---

1. Bigirumwami, *Imana y'Abantu*.
2. Bigirumwami, *Umuntu*.

Mother Tongue as Effective Means of Evangelization Ignored in the Beginning

In *Umuntu*, Bigirumwami points out that in 1980 African theologians met in Yaoundé, Cameroon, for a conference in line with Vatican II. The participants pointed out the importance of the mother tongue, which had been neglected by the earliest missionaries in Africa.

> Abazungu bigishije Ivanjili abanyafurika, bayigisha kizungu, ntiyahuza n'ubwenge bwabo n'umutima wabo. Bati: Noneho nitwigishe Ivanjili mu mvugo abanyegihugu bumva ihuze n'umuco mwiza w'igihugu.[3]

> [The white people evangelized Africans in Western ways; the reason why the gospel did not reach the African intellect and their hearts. The reason why we have to teach and evangelize in languages that the citizens understand so that the gospel will march with the good culture of the country.]

From this African theologians' observation, which is quoted by Bigirumwami, we observe that they came to the realization that "the mother tongue is the vehicle for the primal imagination of African."[4] In order to reach their hearts it was very important to use their heart language so that they may "drink from [their] own wells."[5]

In Rwanda, the Roman Catholic missionaries coming from Tanganyika (Tanzania) and Uganda made the mistake of neglecting the importance of the mother tongue. The Luganda and Swahili languages dominated their writing in the beginning. Laurent Rutinduka indicates that:

> Dès 1902, les missionnaires commencèrent à mener un travail systématique de traductions et de compositions des textes en Kinyarwanda. L'expérience acquise en

3. Bigirumwami, *Umuntu*, 97.
4. Laryea, "Letting the Gospel Re-Shape Culture," 31.
5. Bediako, "Biblical Exegesis in the African Context," 17.

Ouganda et en Tanzanie par les missionnaires et par les
catéchistes devint une base et une bonne leçon pour les
catéchumènes rwandais. Les premiers livres imprimés
au Rwanda pour la catéchèse avaient un langage étrange:
les langues parlées autour du lac Victoria. Le tout premier livre de catéchèse apparut en 1902. Il s'agissait de
l'*Ekitabu kyo kufutura bigambo bye dini okuva ku kulemye bwi si okugera mu misi wacu* (livre qui explique
les paroles de la Religion depuis la création du monde
jusqu'à nos jours).[6]

[From 1902, the missionaries began to carry out a sys-
tematic work of translation and composition of texts
in Kinyarwanda. The experience gained in Uganda and
Tanzania by missionaries and catechists became a foundation and a good lesson for Rwandan catechumens.
The first books printed in Rwanda for catechesis used
a strange language: the languages spoken around Lake
Victoria. The very first catechetical book appeared in
1902. It was the *Ekitabu kyo kufutura bigambo bye dini
okuva ku kulemye bwi si okugera mu misi wacu* (book
that explains the words of the religion from the creation
of the world to our days).]

Rutinduka points out also that *Kifayo*, a catechism manual
prepared by Priest Alphonse Brad at Save, which was a kind of
religious history, was also so difficult to read that later it was abandoned.[7] The Roman Catholic missionaries did not engage themselves in Bible translation in the beginning; for them catechism
teaching was the main focus.[8] In his paper presented during the
Recyclage Sarcerdotal sur Culture Traditionnelle et Christianisme
in 1969, Bigirumwami came across the work of the first missionaries and the use of mixed language or foreign language in Rwanda
and its impact on the gospel.

Au Rwanda, nos premiers évangélisateurs, pères Blancs,
nos pères dans la foi, venant du Buganda et du Tanganika,

6. Rutinduka, «L'Église catholique au Rwanda,» 30.
7. Rutinduka, «L'Église catholique au Rwanda,» 30.
8. Akimana, "Translation Issues," 100.

nous ont enseigné l'Evangile dans une langue mélangée de kiganda, de kiswahili et de kinyarwanda. Des mots inconnus et parfois étranges furent introduits : par ex. « Mungu » = Dieu a la même assonance que « imungu » = charançon et « umwungu » = courge, citrouille! Un bon payen voulant me convaincre et pour que je n'insiste plus sur notre discution, me dit : « Mba ndoga Mwungu! » = que j'empoisonne Dieu ; « Moyo Mutakatifu » pour Esprit saint – on sait que « umwoyo » veut dire anus.[9]

[In Rwanda, our first evangelizers, the white fathers, our fathers in faith, from Buganda and Tanganyika, taught us the gospel in a mixture of Kiganda, Kiswahili, and Kinyarwanda. Unknown and sometimes strange words were introduced: e.g., "*Mungu*" = God, has the same assonance as "*imungu*" = weevil and "*umwungu*" = squash, pumpkin! A good pagan, wanting to convince me that I should no longer insist on discussing with him, told me: "*Mba ndoga Mwungu!*" That I poison God; "*Moyo Mutakatifu*" for Holy Spirit—we know that "*umwoyo*" means anus.]

Bigirumwami indicates that the use of a foreign language did not prevent people from converting to Christianity in Rwanda, Zaire (DR-Congo), where French and Swahili were used, and in Mali, where French was used. He further indicates that:

Le monde de l'Eglise catholique soumis au missel romain et au rituel romain depuis le moyen-âge jusqu'à nos jours, a prié Dieu et a chanté ses louanges en latin ? Dieu seul sait le nombre incalculable d'hommes sanctifies par la liturgie célébrée en latin.[10]

[The world of the Catholic Church, subjected to Roman missal and Roman ritual from the Middle Ages to the present day, prays to God and sings his praises in Latin? God alone knows the incalculable number of men sanctified by the liturgy celebrated in Latin.]

9. Bigirumwami, «Rites, Proverbes, et Fables,» 6.
10. Bigirumwami, "Rites, Proverbes, et Fables," 6.

For Bigirumwami, the use of a lingua franca or foreign language brought many people to Christianity, but led also to a failure to inculturate the gospel and a rejection of the gospel by the elite class in Africa and Asia.[11] Many of the first converts to Christian faith in Rwanda were not strong in their faith because they were not taught in their mother tongue. In the example that Bigirumwami pointed out above, *Mungu*, meaning God, was a borrowed Swahili word. The major problem with the name *Mungu* was not only the similar sound to other Rwandan common words, but also the fact that Rwandans were not afraid to use it indiscriminately, which was impossible with the name *Imana*.

A Rwandan could not say "*Nda karoga Imana*," meaning "May I empoison God," but with *Mungu* it was possible. Instead, a Rwandan would say "*Ndakabura Imana*," "May I lose God"; "*Ndakicwa n'Imanai*," "May I be killed by God." When it comes to poison, a Rwandan would say "*Nda kakuroga*, or" "*Mba nkurugo*," meaning "May I empoison you." At no point would a Rwandan try to suggest that he/she could empoison God, because for Rwandans, *Imana* is a supreme being, beyond human beings; *Imana s'umuntu*, meaning "God is not a human being." With the name *Mungu*, the impossible was possible, because the word was foreign to the Rwandan context.

Moyo Mutakatifu, literally in Swahili "pure heart," is used to denote the Holy Spirit in Kinyarwanda. The word *moyo*[12] *sounds like the Kinyarwanda word mwoyo*, meaning anus. This made the word *moyo* a joke word in Kinyarwanda. Though Swahili is a Bantu language, the language is still dynamic and sounds, form, and meaning differ from one language to another. Later, another Swahili word was borrowed, *roho*,[13] meaning spirit/soul. Yet as Bigirumwami indicates, Rwandans had more than one word that denoted *âme*, meaning soul. For the Rwandan, *ubwenge*, meaning

11. Bigirumwami, "Rites, Proverbes, et Fables," 6–7.

12. *Moyo*: "(1) the heart (the physical organ); (2) the heart, feeling, soul, mind, will, self . . ." Johnson, *Standard Swahili-English Dictionary*, 296.

13. *Roho* meaning "soul, spirit, life, vital principle . . ." Johnson, *Standard Swahili-English Dictionary*, 400–401.

intelligence, and *umutima*, meaning will, were the equivalent of soul. *Umutima* has two meanings: it denotes the physical part (heart) and also the moral part (will, conscience). When someone dies, Rwandans would say *"Avuyemo umwuka or araciye,"* meaning that the spirit is gone, or there is a cutoff between the *umutima n'ubwnege* (soul) and the *umubiri* (body). For a Rwandan to stop breathing means a separation between the body and the soul. In his analysis, Bigirumwami came to the conclusion that "âme [soul] = roho" is the spirit which gives life to the body, and when it is departed the body became a corpse.[14] Rwandans believed in life after death, which was why when someone died they would not call him/her so-and-so spirit, but rather they would say *"umuzimu wa . . . ,"* meaning the ghost of . . .[15] He further indicates that: *"Abanyarwanda, koko bemera ko umubili w'umuntu ubamo ikintu cyalemwe n'Imana, kigira umuntu agisamwa, kugeza igihe cyo gupfa, ndetse kigakomeza kubaho amaze gupfa"*[16] [Truly, Rwandans believe that a human is made of something created by God which makes him/her human from conception till death, and which continues to exist after death]. For Rwandans the spirit is more about breath, and plays a remarkable role in separating the *ubwenge n'umutima* (soul) and *umubiri* (body). Because they had not been able to grasp the Rwandan understanding of soul, the Roman Catholic missionaries borrowed the Swahili words *moyo* and *roho* and used them as loan words in Kinyarwanda.

German missionaries, headed by Ernst Johanssen and Karl Roehl, initiated the work of Bible translation among the Protestants. Instead of translating from Swahili to Kinyarwanda, they started by working on Kinyarwanda orthography, and then embarked on translation.[17] German Lutheran missionaries headed by Johanssen launched the work of creating a "church language" close to the Rwandan worldview.[18] Thus, words taken from everyday life of

14. Bigirumwami, *Imana y'Abantu*, 20.

15. Bigirumwami, *Imana y'Abantu*, 20.

16. Bigirumwami, *Imana y'Abantu*, 21.

17. Akimana, "Translation Issues," 92–93.

18. Spijker, "Is Pagan Dead?," 5.

Rwandans, like *Imana* for God, *Umwuka Wera* for Holy Ghost, and *itorero* for church, were adopted by the church.[19]

In 1957, when the whole Bible in Kinyarwanda, *Bibiliya Yera*, was published,[20] the name *Imana* was not replaced; *Umwuka Wera*, literally "white air," was used in referring to Holy Spirit, and *ubugingo* was used in referring to the soul. The concept of *Umwuka Wera* for the Holy Spirit brought confusion due to fact that it is not easy to explain to Rwandans the color of the air. Why "white spirit"? Was it due to the expression *kwera*, used in divination, or *kwera* as a white color? Deep research is needed here to determine why German Lutheran missionaries and the *Bibiliya Yera* translators chose to use the word *wera*, which may mean white. But in teaching catechism in most of the Protestant churches in Rwanda, the idea of color is foremost. White represents purity. The concept of *Umwuka Wera* for the Holy Spirit is explained in that way, referring to purity, holiness.

Concerning the issue of mother tongue and Bible translation in Rwanda, the Protestants produced the Bible in Kinyarwanda before the Kinyarwanda orthography had been stabilized. The German Lutheran missionaries who started working on a "church language" closer to Rwandan context left the country before being able to complete their work.[21] Gabriel Akimana indicates that the *Bibiliya Yera* produced by Protestants was revised to meet the new orthography promulgated in a ministerial decree of 1986.[22] For Roman Catholics, it took more than ninety years to produce the whole Bible in Kinyarwanda, meaning that many of the borrowed words and coined ones were contextualized. Missionaries who neglected the use of the mother tongue in the beginning with Bible translation came to realize its importance. Lamin Sanneh, in discussing West African Christianity, points out that:

> Missionaries from the West, aware of the significance of the local springs of religious vitality, could no longer

19. Spijker, "Is Pagan Dead?," 5..

20. Akimana, "Translation Issues," 92–100.

21. Spijker, "Is Pagan Dead?," 5.

22. Akimana, "Translation Issues," 100.

dispense with African agents and would themselves have to clothe their thinking in the indigenous culture if their endeavours were to bear any fruit. Thus it came about that serious attention was paid to the urgency of using African workers and to the case for developing African languages.[23]

Both Roman Catholic missionaries and Protestant missionaries later realized the importance of mother tongue use, and they played a remarkable role in developing the education sector in Rwanda. As indicated by Lamin Sanneh, Africans were used in developing African languages. In Rwanda, Roman Catholic missionaries used the first seminarians in developing Kinyarwanda orthography. For Bigirumwami, the neglect of mother tongue usage and the demonization of African traditions by the first Western missionaries did not lead to a lack of inculturation of the gospel only, but also accentuated the adage "errare humanum est," meaning "to err is human."[24] For Bigirumwami, it is not worth spending time discussing the mistakes committed by first Western missionaries, but rather one should move on and work on incarnating the gospel in Rwanda and Africa in general.

Bigirumwami and Advocacy of Mother Tongue Use

In his article "Letting the Gospel Re-Shape Culture: Theological Creativity in Mother Tongue," Philip T. Laryea indicates that "up to now most scholars in Africa still write and do theology in European languages."[25] In explaining the reason given by John Pobee, he indicates that "Pobee gives two reasons why theologians in Africa write in European languages: first, because it is convenient to do so, and second because it allows for a wide readership. By convenience, I presume he means the relative ease way with which one may have access to documentation in those language and the technology of

23. Sanneh, *West African Christianity*, 103.
24. Bigirumwami, «Rites, Proverbes et Fables,» 6.
25. Laryea, "Letting the Gospel Re-Shape Culture," 27.

which makes such documentation possible."[26] For Laryea, though well placed, the languages of empire builders are not well equipped to convey the realities of the African situation.[27]

What Laryea discussed in his article in 2001 Bigirumwami had already noticed in 1960s, and he started advocating for mother tongue use. Kinyarwanda helped Bigirumwami in understanding and appreciating the value of Rwandan traditions for Christian faith. Bigirumwami did not engage himself in a scholarly discussion on the importance of mother tongue; rather, knowing its importance, he wrote his entire books in Kinyarwanda. A few articles were published in French by Bigirumwami, and some letters and summaries of chapters for non-Kinyarwanda readers. In one of his letters to his brothers in the priesthood, introducing his books, Bigirumwami wrote:

> Je recommande ce recueil de recherches si variées à l'attention des pasteurs d'âmes (prêtres), des éducateurs (religieux, religieuses, instituteurs et institutrices, moniteurs et monitrices, catéchistes.) A présent, tous, vous aurez l'occasion, au moyen de cet in[s]trument sic, de vous initier au style et au génie de la langue, aux usages et coutumes profanes et religieus . . . Tout ce que vous trouvez dans ce recueil trahit le fond de l'âme et du cœur du munyarwanda. Profitez de cette occasion de vous approcher du munyarwanda, parlant comme lui et avec lui, après avoir pense comme lui. Vous avez une mine inépuisable de la richesse linguistique et coutumière du Rwanda ancien et nouveau.[28]

> [I recommend this collection of such varied research to the attention of pastors of souls (priests), educators (religious men and women, teachers, instructors, and catechists). Now all of you will have the opportunity by means of this instrument to initiate yourselves into the style and genius of the language, to the secular and religious practices and customs . . . All that you find in this

26. Laryea, "Letting the Gospel Re-Shape Culture," 27.

27. Laryea, "Letting the Gospel Re-Shape Culture," 27.

28. Bigirumwami, «A mes Frères dans le Sacerdoce.»

collection reveals the heart and soul of munyarwanda. Take this opportunity to approach the munyarwanda, speaking like him and with him, after thinking like him. You have an inexhaustible rich mine of language and custom of ancient and modern Rwanda.]

Bigirumwami described his collection of Rwandan traditions, rites, and practices as a rich and inexhaustible linguistic and cultural mine. He urges those in ministry, education, and leadership to use it. The different people that Bigirumwami mentioned above had to think like a munyarwanda (Rwandan), and the language was the vehicle to help them approach a munyarwanda and be able to speak like him/her with him/her. Having experienced the problem of ineffective communication,[29] Bigirumwami was concerned for the young, priests, educators, and leaders. He desired that his collection be made available for them, especially when starting their intellectual training, so that it could help in their intellectual, moral, psychological, and religious formation.[30] Bigirumwami wanted his readers not just to read and understand munyarwanda; he wanted his collection to be used in all aspects of life. "Lisez ce recueil, comprenez-le, au besoin apprenez-en des expressions par cœur; utilisez-le dans vos conversations, vos expressions, dans vos sermons et conférences, dans vos agissements"[31] [Read this collection, understand it, if necessary learn it by heart; use it in your conversations, your expressions, in your sermons and conferences, in your actions]. The books were not for relaxation; rather, the collection on Rwandan traditions had to be in the hearts and on lips of everyone engaged in the ministry in Rwanda. The country's leaders were asked to encourage the good usage of our ancestors's legacy.[32]

Bigirumwami's concern for the young to know their mother tongue, and use it in their education in general, brought the idea of starting a journal for primary pupils in Rwanda, called

29. Bigirumwami, *Umuntu*, 10.

30. Bigirumwami, «A mes Frères dans le Sacerdoce.»

31. Bigirumwami, «A mes Frères dans le Sacerdoce.»

32. Bigirumwami, «A mes Frères dans le Sacerdoce.»

Hobe. According to Gapfizi Felicien, editor of *Hobe* from 1996 to October 2018, when the interview was conducted, "*Hobe* was started by Bishop Bigirumwami Aloys, with the following objectives: Inform, Educate, Recreation and Evangelize youth based on the human and Christian values."[33] In its history section, the online news paper *Kanyarwanda* published a short biography on Bigirumwami Aloys. They indicate that:

> In December 1954 he founded the magazine *Hobe* for youth. *Hobe*, written entirely in Kinyarwanda, was a great success. It was part of a deliberate effort to rehabilitate the Rwandan culture in an age where it was common to dismiss the culture as inferiod [*sic*] to western civilization. Bigirumwami wrote many books on the Rwandan culture. He was a strong believer in unity among the Rwandan people, and criticized foreign publications that exaggerated the differences between the different groups.[34]

From this quotation it is clear Bigirumwami was concerned about the young people who were in the same situation as he had been when he was young. Starting *Hobe* was one of his contributions to the education of young people about Rwandan culture. Consequently, Kinyarwanda was a very important vehicle for young Rwandans to get to know their culture. At school students were taught in French while Kinyarwanda was learned as a language course. *Hobe* brought historical and cultural education in Kinyarwanda to the young. Although *Hobe* was written in Kinyarwanda, Gapfizi indicates that "for education there were also sections written in Kinyarwanda with translation in French to teach French."[35] French was not neglected by *Hobe*, as it was the medium of education in schools at the time. *Hobe* was not the only journal started by Bigirumwami; he launched other journals adapted to the level of the population, like *Bene Urugo* for families and *Asanase* for seminarians and novices' parents.[36] Bigirumwami

33. Felicien Gapfizi, interview, July 10, 2018, Kigali.
34. Kanyarwanda, "Aloys Bigirumwami."
35. Gapfizi, interview.
36. Editions du Secrétariat général de la CEPR, *Hommage a Mgr Aloys*

was greatly concerned for the family; in 1962 he founded Action Catholique des Foyers (AGI), meaning Catholic Action of Households. The objective of AGI was to promote material and spiritual development of couples.[37] *Cum Paraclito*, launched in 1965 in the context of Vatican II, was for intellectuals. In 1970 the journal was renamed *Revue Foi et Culture* so that it could take on the continuity of the Recyclage Sacerdotal of 1969. After the resignation of Bishop Aloys Bigirumwami in 1974, the journal ceased publication.[38] This indicates how much impact he had in the articles published in the journal, as it dealt with gospel and culture. After him the subject was not of the same importance for his successors, and this is one of the reasons why the process of inculturation did not continue well after Bigirumwami.

Though Bigirumwami advocated for mother tongue usage in Rwanda and Africa in general, he pointed out in the 1980s that he was not happy with the fact that the Western languages were still in use. For him it was not good that even after independence in Zaire, currenty DR-Congo, a Swahili and French catechism was still in use, whereas in Rwandan schools religion was taught in French, not in Kinyarwanda.[39] You may ask why Bigirumwami was not happy with the use of Swahili in evangelizing Congolese. There is a scholarly debate on Swahili as a foreign language, a mix of Arab, Hindu, European languages and Bantu languages. Assibi Apatewon Amidu discusses the debate on Kiswahili in his article "Kiswahili: People, Language, Literature and Lingua Franca."[40] What we cannot ignore is the fact that there are people in East Africa for whom Swahili is their mother tongue, but for the majority it is not. Concerning DR-Congo, Helena Lopez Palma

---

Bigirumwami, 41.

37. Editions du Secrétariat général de la CEPR, *Hommage a Mgr Aloys Bigirumwami*, 47.

38. Editions du Secrétariat général de la CEPR, *Hommage a Mgr Aloys Bigirumwami*, 64.

39. Bigirumwami, *Umuntu*, 97.

40. Amidu, "Kiswahili, "104–23.

indicates that the country has 214 native languages.[41] This shows that Bigirumwami was concerned for those millions of Congolese who were not able to hear the gospel or to learn the catechism in their mother tongue. He was unhappy with the fact that in Rwanda religion was being taught in French. Bigirumwami was among those who might have played a remarkable role in pushing for the teaching of religion in secondary schools in Kinyarwanda, because he took up the task of writing to show that it was not good to teach religion in French only. Yet the church and the Rwandan government in the education sector continued in the line of promoting the colonizers' languages and culture while undermining Kinyarwanda, and as result Rwandan culture was relegated to the second place.

Bigirumwami and Rwandan Primal Religion

In 1962 Bigirumwami started publishing his collections on Rwandan culture. It was not easy for him to come to that point of being able to express publicly and in print his ideas on religion and culture considered as "paganism" at the time. How Bigirumwami was able to come to the understanding of Rwandan primal religion as the foundation of Rwandan Christian faith is the main point that I wish to discuss in this section.

Imana y'abantu–Imana mu bantu—Natural Revelation and Special Revelation

Bigirumwami points out in his book *Umuntu* that on September 24–29, 1980, theologians attending a conference declared in line with Vatican II that:

> Ibyahishuliwe Umulyango w'Abayahudi, bitahishwe abandi bantu bazi neza amategeko y'Imana, kuko yandi-tse mu mitima yabo. Bityo Jambo w'Imana akaba yihishe

---

41. Palma, "Aspects of Multilingualism," 1.

mu migenzo no mu mvugo karande (culture traditio-
nelle) y'abantu mu bihugu batuyemo.[42]

[What was revealed to Jews was not hidden from other
people who know the laws of God, which are written in
their hearts. Therefore, the Word of God [meaning Jesus]
is hidden in traditions and expressions (traditional culture) of people in the countries where they live.]

The declaration did not only point out that Africans had
known God before the arrival of Western missionaries, but also indicated the fact that Jesus was already in Africa, hidden in African
traditions. In his earliest book, *Imana y'abantu, Abantu b'Imana,
Imana mu Bantu, Abantu mu Mana* [God of People, People of
God, God among People, People in God], meaning "God Creator
and Redeemer," Bigirumwami discussed natural revelation and
special Revelation. The first part of the book focused on *Imana
y'Abantu–Abantu b'Imana* [God the creator].

Muli aka gatabo, ndashaka kuvuga ko abantu bose, iyo
bava bakagera, batewemo, UMUTIMA n'UBWENGE
by'IMANA. Abantu bose, banze bakunze, muli roho
yabo no mu mubuli wabo, bahasanga Imana yabakuye
mu busa bakabaho; bagasanga baliho batibeshejeho,
ahubwo babeshejweho n'IYABAREMYE.[43]

[In this small book, I want to say that in all people, wherever there are, the HEART and INTELLIGENCE of GOD
were planted in them. All people, whether they refuse or
accept it, in their soul and body, they found God, who created them from nothing, and they existed and the CRE-
ATOR is the one who sustains them in their lives.]

The conference declaration about natural revelation confirmed what Bigirumwami had already discussed above. For Bigirumwami, though all people know God, they differ when talking
about God: "*Hali abantu bavugako ni nabo benshi cyane bavuga
ko 'IMANA ali iy'ABANTU – ABANTU bakaba ab'IMANA'. Hali*

42. Bigirumwami, *Umuntu*, 97.
43. Bigirumwami, *Imana y'Abantu*, 5.

abantu bitwa "ABAKRISTU" bungamo bavuga ngo: IMANA iba mu BANTU- ABANTU bakaba mu MANA."[44] [There are people who say that, and they are the majority, "GOD is God of PEOPLE—PEOPLE are People of GOD." There are others called "CHRISTIANS" who add: GOD dwells among PEOPLE—PEOPLE dwell in GOD.] For Bigirumwami, the first category is made up of those people who know the existence of God but have not heard about the gospel of Jesus. The second category is made of Christians who had the understanding of God living among them through the incarnation of Jesus Christ.[45]

Discussing the first category of people, *Imana y'Abantu–Abantu b'Imana*, meaning those who know God the Creator, he noted, *"tuvuge ko abantu bose bemera Imana, aliko uko bayivuga n'uko bayiyambaza bili ukundi: bamwe ukwabo abandi ukwabo, bagasa na ba bandi basara, aliko bakagusha ku ijambo limwe: 'Imana.'"*[46] [we may say that all people believe in God, but the way they talk and call up on him differs: some have their different ways, others theirs, and they are like those who out of their madness will end up with one word: 'God.'"] He further indicates, *"Nitumenye ko Abakristu bemera kandi bazi Ivanjili batali mu bahuzagulika bavuga Imana. Abo ni abali mu Kliziya ya Yesu, imwe, ntagatifu, Gatolika (ya hose, ya bose), kandi ikomoka ku Ntumwa."*[47] [Let us know that the Christians who believe and understand the gospel are not among those who are not stable in talking about God. Those are the ones in the church of Jesus, one, holy, catholic (of everywhere, of everyone), which originated from the apostles.] Bigirimwami thus distinguished between the first category of people and Christians. Bigirumwami was able to demonstrate how all people deep in their hearts do know that God exists, though their knowledge is limited, which is the reason why it is important to move on to the understanding of God living among people for full revelation. The first category of people naturally know that God exists but Christians

44. Bigirumwami, *IMana y'Abantu*, 5.
45. Bigirumwami, *Imana y'Abantu*, 6.
46. Bigirumwami, *Imana y'Abantu*, 13.
47. Bigirumwami, *Imana y'Abantu*, 13.

have come to the true understanding of God through special revelation, which is the incarnation of Jesus.

It is noteworthy to point out that even among Christians, for Bigirumwami only those who are in the Holy Catholic Church are the ones who do not change in their beliefs.

> Hali abemera Ivanjili ya Jambo wigize Umuntu, aliko bagacisha ukubili na Petero yashinze abamwemera. Yezu yaramubwiye ati: "Uli urutare, kuli urwo rutare, ni ho nzubaka Kliziya yanjye" (Mat.16, 18).[48]

> [There are those who accept the gospel of the Word, who became a human, but they veer away from Peter, whom Jesus made responsible for the believers. Jesus told him: "You are the rock, on that rock; I will build my Church (Matt 16:18).]

For Bigirumwami, only Christians from the Roman Catholic Church are part of the church of Jesus. He indicates that "*Abo muri Kliziya Gatolika 'Abagatoliki', nibo ba Yezu, nibo Yezu yasigiye Petero 'urutare y'ubatseho Kliliziya ye'*" [Those who are in the Catholic Church, "Catholics," are the ones belonging to Jesus, are the ones that Jesus left to Peter, "the rock that the church is built on."] Thus, for Bigirumwami, there are three types of Christians: Catholics, those separated with Roman Catholic Church due to misunderstanding from 800–1054 (Orthodox), and the Protestants, who do not accept the pope. He further points out four factors that indicate a true church: unity, holiness, being universal (catholic), and originating from the apostles. After explaining those four factors, he clearly concludes that you cannot find any of the four factors among Orthodox and Protestants but only within the Roman Catholic Church, headed by the pope. For him, if one wants to argue against this, one should visit Rome, Saint Peter's Cathedral, and the pope, in order to understand that the Roman Catholic Church is the only church that originates from the apostles.[49]

---

48. Bigirumwami, *Imana y'Abantu*, 13.

49. Bigirumwami, *Imana y'Abantu*, 54–57.

Bigirumwami's ecclesiology was influenced by the Vatican II definition of the church. In defining the church, Vatican II concluded that "the church is at one and the same time 'a visible structure' and 'the mystical body of Christ.'" Kevin Giles indicates that Vatican II stressed the visible structure part of the church, which Jesus Christ handed over to Peter and the apostles and their successor bishops.[50] This view has limitations, as the New Testament does not point out that Jesus called into being the church as a hierarchically ordered and clearly structured institutional society.[51] Another reason is the fact that a historical explanation of the visible church cannot help define the invisible church of Jesus Christ, and even church leaders do not agree on that history. Giles further indicates that defining the church was not one of the topics that the early church dealt with. It was during the Reformation that Protestants and Roman Catholics attempted to define the church, and the result was the launch of competing assertions as there was no agreement on the definition.[52] Some definitions Giles lists are: "the church, the divinely constituted institution called into being by Christ"[53]; "the church, the body of Christ"[54]; "the people of God"[55]; "the church, Christians working in the world"[56]; "the church as congregation"; and "the church, the Christian community."[57] From these we notice that Bigirumwami's understanding of church is in line with the first given here, which was stressed by Vatican II. Two different Greek words are used in reference to the "rock" named by Jesus in Matthew 16:18. Commenting on the verse, the *Wycliffe Bible Commentary* indicates that "there is an obvious play upon the words Peter (Petros, proper

---

50. Giles, *What on Earth Is the Church?* 8.

51. Giles, *What on Earth Is the Church?*, 8.

52. Giles, *What on Earth Is the Church?*, 1.

53. Giles, *What on Earth Is the Church?*, 8.

54. Giles, *What on Earth Is the Church?*, 9.

55. Giles, *What on Earth Is the Church?*, 11.

56. Giles, *What on Earth Is the Church?*, 12.

57. Giles, *What on Earth Is the Church?*, 15.

name denoting a piece of rock) and rock (Petra, a rocky mass)."[58] The commentary further indicates that "the spiritual body, the church, mentioned here for the first time, is built upon the divinely revealed fact about Christ confessed by Peter (I Cor 3:11; I Peter 2:4). From the given verse the foundation is Jesus Christ. Matthew Henry confirms that by indicating that, 'the word translated "rock" is not the same word as Peter, but is of a similar meaning."[59] He further indicated that it is wrong to consider that Christ meant that Peter is the rock, the foundation of the church.[60] For him, "without doubt Christ himself is the Rock, the tried foundation of the church; and woe to him that attempts to lay any other!"[61] We cannot reject the fact that the church is build on the apostles, Peter included (Ephesians 2:20), but one should not give Peter the power that he doesn't have by making him the foundation. Peter himself pointed out the fact that Jesus Christ is the foundation of the church (1 Pet 2:6), confirming Henry's point.

It is good that Bigirumwami agrees to the fact that all Christians, even those he is considering as not part of Jesus Christ's church, all use the Bible. He further quotes one Protestant thinker who said, "'La Bible fermée nous unit: *Bibliya ibumbye tuyihuriraho twese*. La Bible ouverte nous déunit [*sic*]: *Bibliya ibumbuye iradutandukanya*.'[62] [The closed Bible unites us: *Bibliya ibumbye tuyihuriraho twese*. The open Bible disunites us: *Bibliya ibumbuye iradutandukanya*.]"[63] Commenting on the quotation, Bigirumwami indicates that this is due to the fact that there are many interpretations of the Bible, making the Bible say what it does not say. He clearly indicates that Catholics have chosen to follow the teachings of the pope, and of bishops who are also following the gospel of Jesus and the heroes of the gospel, with a view to avoiding those

---

58. Pfeiffer and Harrison, *Wycliffe Bible Commentary*, 959.

59. Henry, *Commentary on the Whole Bible*, 700.

60. Henry, *Commentary on the Whole Bible*, 700.

61. Henry, *Commentary on the Whole Bible*, 700.

62. Bigirumwami, *Imana y'Abantu*, 58.

63. Bigirumwami, *Imana y'Abantu*, 58.

wrong interpretations of the Bible.[64] What Bigirumwami drew from the quotation is the fact that Protestants allow many people to have access to Bible, leading to false interpretations and imposing their views on the Bible. But he could not see the other side: that he was imposing his Catholic view on the Bible through his own interpretation of Matthew 16:18, in identifying Jesus' words with the Roman Catholic Church.

It was very important to discuss Bigirumwami's ecclesiology as for him those Christians handed over to Peter (Roman Catholics) are the only ones who had received the special revelation that God dwells among them. Thus, it was important to critically assess Bigirumwami's interpretations in order to point out that special revelation is for all Christians, not only Roman Catholic Church members. Though considering Roman Catholics as the only true members of Jesus Christ's church, Bigirumwami further acknowledges that in Rwanda there are other Christians who teach the gospel. He points to Protestants and few Orthodox members, whom he calls to come back to the one church and one leader.[65] Surprisingly, nowhere does Bigirumwami indicate that the gospel preached by Protestants and Orthodox is corrupt or call upon Rwandans not to follow their teachings. Therefore, I consider that his interpretation of Matthew 16:18 was one-sided, due to fact that the Bible does not tell us that human beings have the right and the power to nominate those who are part of Jesus' universal church and have a monopoly on special revelation.

In concluding on the *Imana y'Abantu–Abantu b'Imana*, the people from the first category, Bigirumwami indicates that they are "pagan," by which he means:

> Hali Abapagani batigeze bumva Ivanjili ivugwa, ABATA-RABATIJWE. Abapagani bemera Imana, bakamenya ibyiza n'ibibi, bakamenya ko badapfa. Bitwa Abapagani, kuko batemezwa na Jambo Imana yivugiye ubwayo mu Gitabo Gitagatifu, "Bibliya y'Isezerano lishya."[66]

64. Bigirumwami, *Imana y'Abantu*, 58.
65. Bigirumwami, *Imana y'Abantu*, 84–87.
66. Bigirumwami, *Imana y'Abantu*, 13.

[There are pagans who did not hear the gospel, WHO
WERE NOT BAPTIZED. There are pagans who accept
God, and know right and wrong, and accept the fact that
they are immortal. They are called pagan because they
are not convinced by the Word of God, who speaks in the
Holy Book, "the New Testament Bible."]

Bigirumwami includes all non-Christian religious followers
among the "pagans" when describing why the members of Juda-
ism are also "pagans." According to him, it is because they did
not accept the Word of God (Jesus) and still hold on the Old Testament prophecies fulfilled in the New Testament.[67] Since Bigirumwami himself pointed out that some of the so-called pagans
had not heard the gospel of Jesus, it is not clear why he should
describe them together with those he clearly indicates as having
rejected the gospel of Jesus.

In summary, for Bigirumwami all human beings know that
God exists, and there is no need to debate about that. But few
people had the knowledge that God dwelt among them and they
in him at the time that he was writing. Those are Christians, who
came to that realization through hearing the gospel of Jesus.
Therefore, for Bigirumwami, in the process of evangelization it
is good to take note of the fact that people know God, they know
that there is life after death, and they know to distinguish good
from evil. Bernardin Muzungu, Rwandan priest, historian, and
theologian, is one of few people who lived and worked with both
Alexis Kagame and Aloys Bigirumwami. Standing on the shoulders of these two great Rwandan scholars, Muzungu is a leading
historian and theologian of inculturation in Rwanda. Discussing
Bigirumwami's knowledge, Muzungu, who was a seminarian at
the time of the ordination of Bigirumwami as bishop and presented a poem, later indicated:

A lire attentivement ces écrits de Mgr BIGIRUMWAMI,
surtout en ce qui concerne l'existence d'Imana et son
intime communication avec lui, on se demande où il a
puisé cette connaissance? Pour ceux qui l'ont fréquenté

67. Bigirumwami, *Imana y'Abantu*, 13–14.

et je suis parmi eux, Mgr BIGIRUMWAMI a puisé cette connaissance dans deux sources. La première est la prière, surtout devant le Saint Sacrement devant lequel il passait des heures, surtout dans la discrétion de la nuit. A cela s'ajoute son ministère de contact avec les gens, surtout les pauvres, auquel il faisait beaucoup de biens. Ces deux actes semblent lui avoir donné un sens de comprendre ce que les ordinaires que nous sommes perçoivent à peine.[68]

[To read carefully these writings of Mgr. BIGIRUM-WAMI, especially concerning the existence of *Imana* and his close communication with him, one wonders where he drew this knowledge. For those who attended him, and I am among them, Bishop BIGIRUMWAMI drew this knowledge from two sources. The first is prayer, especially before the Blessed Sacrament, before which he spent hours, especially in the hiddenness of the night. Added to this is his ministry of contact with the people, especially the poor, among whom he did much good. These two acts seem to have given him a sense of understanding what we, the ordinary priests, barely perceive.]

Bigirumwami's books *Imana y'Abantu, Abantu b'Imana* and *Umuntu* were written after Bigirumwami's progressive conversion in understanding primal religion, which I have discussed in the second chapter and in this chapter. But it is true that the first question that anyone who knows the Rwandan context will raise when reading Bigirumwami's books is: Where did he get such great knowledge? I will therefore take into consideration Muzungu's two factors and add a third, which is reading culture. Throughout Bigirumwami's books you will notice that he had a reading culture. He uses books, journals, newspapers, conference reports, and letters in his writings.

---

68. Muzungu, «Centenaire du Clergé Rwandais,» 45.

Rwandan Beliefs and Life beyond Death

Bigirumwami's discussion of the spread of Christianity in Rwanda by the white fathers indicates that before their arrival Rwandans knew God. The evidence for this is found in the names given to *Imana*, names given to people, and in proverbs.[69] Apart from believing in God, Rwandans also knew about the continuation of life after death. This was due to their belief in *Abazimu*,[70] meaning spirits of the dead. For Rwandans, the *Abazimu* could attack their family members. According to Bigirumwami, this is the fact of the relationship between the dead and living.[71] Bigirumwami further indicates that when Rwandans neglected their dead they encountered different problems in their lives. As a result, they developed some rites and a cult, *Kuraguza*, which serves to identify the deceased family member who is not happy in order to appease him/her. *Guterekera* is to bring back to a good mood a spirit who is angry by trying to make him/her smile by saying "*Seka seka, gororoka,*" meaning "Smile smile, be straight

69. Bigirumwami, *Imana y'Abantu*, 18–19.

70. «Qu'est-ce un *Muzimu*? C'est un défunt dans la conception des rwandais la mort d'un homme n'est pas sa réduction au néant. Le défunt signifie littéralement l'éteint. L'éteint est ce qui est brulé mais laisse des cendres et les cendres sont quelque choses. En langage symbolique, le *Muzimu* (l'éteint) est la cendre que laisse un homme qui meurt. Dans l'imagination de nos ancêtres le cadavre n'a pas d'ombre par ce que le *Muzimu* est justement cette ombre dite *igicucu*. Apres la mort, les défunts habitent dans l'outre–tombe appelé *Ikuzimu*. Ce qui pousse les Rwandais a croire que l'homme mort n'est pas réduit au néant, reste un mystère. Ce désir d'une vie sempiternelle est probablement la cause de la fusion entre le désir et la réalité.» [What is a *Muzimu*? It is a deceased person in Rwandans' conception. The death of a man does not mean he is reduced to nothingness. The deceased literally means 'extinguished.' The extingushed is what is burned but leaves ashes and ashes are significant. In symbolic language, the *Muzimu* (the extinguished) is the ash left by a man who dies. In the imagination of our ancestors the corpse has no shadow because the *Muzimu* is precisely this shadow called *igicucu*. After death, the deceased live in the grave called *Ikuzimu* (underground). What drives Rwandans to believe that the dead man is not reduced to nothing remains a mystery. This desire for an eternal life is probably the cause of the fusion between desire and reality.] Muzungu, «Religion Traditionnelle des Rwandais,» 9.

71. Bigirumwami, *Imana y'Abantu*, 20–21.

[come down]." *Kubandwa* was used when people continued to face problems, or succumb to successive diseases, on account of the fact that the *Abazimu* did not accept being appeased in this way. Therefore, people approach the high and powerful spirit of Lyangombe through the *kubandwa*, because they believe that he is the one to end the problems that they are going through.[72] Bigirumwami saw nothing wrong in what they were doing, as it shows that they really believed in life after death, though they could not know where people were going after death.[73]

Rwandan Rites and Taboos According to Bigirumwami

Rwandans had also their traditions, rites, and taboos before the arrival of colonizers and Western missionaries. For Bigirumwami, "*Nta gihugu kilimo abantu kibura ubulyo bwo kubabanya. Ubwo bulyo ni umuco, ni ingiro, ni ibyo bazira kuvuga no gukora.*"[74] [There is no country with people that does not have the ways of helping them live together. Those ways consist in culture, rites, and what is forbidden to say or to do.] With respect to Rwanda, Bigirumwami noticed three important aspects to these customs. Firstly, Rwandans have good practices in educating their children, creativity in husbandry, and good marriage customs and burial ceremonies.[75] Secondly, there are what Bigirumwami called "intimidations," those ways of compelling people to live together. For him, if anyone were to remove intimidations from traditions, rites, and taboos, which say "*Uramutse udakoze ibi nti wa byara*" [You cannot give birth if you don't do this], "*Nti wakira ngo ukungahare*" [You cannot be wealthy], "*Ntabwo wapfa [wambaye iyi mpigi]*" [You cannot die if you are wearing this amulet]; it may not be wrong. Thirdly, Bigirumwami indentified problematic elements in Rwandan ways: "*Ikindi gihinyuka cyane cyo mu bulyo*

72. Bigirumwami, *Imana y'Abantu*, 20–21.

73. Bigirumwami, *Imana y'Abantu*, 21.

74. Bigirumwami, *Imana y'Abantu*, 22

75. Bigirumwami, *Imana y'Abantu*, 21.

bw'abanyarwanda, ni ugukora no kuvuga ibitagira agaciro, bitagira ihuliro n'ibyo babona n'ibyo bumva"[76] [Another questionable aspect of Rwandan ways is to do and to say things with no value, which do not agree with what they see and hear]. Bigirumwami points out some examples:

> Kwiyambaza impigi n'inzaratsi, aho kwivuza indwara wiyambaza abazi kuvura, aho kugisha inama itunganye. Kwemera uburozi bw'ubutererano, no kwemera abahuzi n'abashora. Kugangahurwa ngo utazakubitwa n'inkuba, kwemera ko bazinga abakobwa ntibasabwe; ko bamanika abagore ntibasame inda, ntibabyare. Kwemera ko abatirabuye bapfushije umuntu bahumana; ko umugabo yapfushije umugore cyangwa umugore yapfushije umugabo, ngo batejejwe urupfu rwabakulikirana. N'ibindi nk'ibyo by'abanyabwenge buke, butibaza ngo bwisubize, by'abanyabwenge buke bapfa kuvuga, ngo ni ko abandi bavuga, bapfa gukora ibyo bakora; ngo ni ko abandi bakora, ngo ni ko abandi babiziriliza.[77]

[Using amulets when they are sick, instead of looking out for people to treat their sickness, and seeking for good advice. To accept the fact that someone can trap or send poison to harm them, to believe what the *abahuzi n'abashoro* (mediators/diviners) tells them. To accept the rite of purifying someone so that he/she will not be struck by lightning; to believe that girls can be prevented from getting pregnant and giving birth; that women are prevented to the extent of not conceiving and not giving birth. To believe that when the rite of *kwirabura* is not carried out after death, they may be unclean; that when a man loses his wife or the wife loses her husband, if they do not carry out the rite of *kwirabura*, death can keep pursuing them. And other such things of uncivilized people (literally, "people with little knowledge"), who just say, it is what other are saying; they just do what they do, saying that it is how others are doing it; it is according to our taboos.]

76. Bigirumwami, *Imana y'Abantu*, 22.
77. Bigirumwami, *Imana y'Abantu*, 22–23.

Accepting the above practices was for Bigirumwami to be *umunyabwenge buke*. There is no exact word in English, but it means someone with little knowledge. He did not call it *ubugoryi* (nonsense) or *ubupfu* (foolishness). For him, the above beliefs were the negative side of pre-colonial Rwandan traditions, which the gospel of Jesus Christ had to redeem. But, as pointed it out in the second chapter, the gospel was spread in Rwanda by totally opposing it to Rwandan pre-colonial tradition.

Mungu and Imana in Rwanda

As noted earlier, on their arrival Roman Catholic missionaries refused to use the word *Imana* for God; they rather used *Mungu*. Vellah Temko Ngaina indicates that "the process of translation does not imply a simple substitution of one concept for another, but rather an engagement that finds its grounding in the process of translation."[78] She further points out that "this engagement recognizes the fact that underlying these cultural and religious divides are primal worldviews that play a major role."[79] The use of *Mungu* instead of *Imana* amounted to replacement of an indigenous term with a borrowed concept within a receptor culture because the missionaries were not engaging with it so as to understand its concept of *Imana*. Bigirumwami points out that they had the following reason: the Rwandan God (*Imana*) was seen by the first Western missionaries as *amahirwe*: luck/chance; this was due to the fact that Rwandans in their everyday life use *na gize Imana*, meaning "I had God," and *naka ya gize Imana*, meaning "so has God." Therefore, for them *Imana* was not to be considered in denoting God. The second reason was that it was due to the fact that Rwandan ancestors use to wear *imana yeze*, which was a sacred object, but for Bigirumwami the white fathers arriving in Rwanda were doing something similar in wearing rosaries with the cross of Christ on them. The ceremony of offering rosaries to

78. Ngaina, "Bible Translation," 24.
79. Ngaina, "Bible Translation," 24.

Christians was accompanied by words of incantation, which was similar to the Rwandan rite of *kubandwa* when the words of incantation followed the wearing of *imana yeze*.[80] For, Bigirumwami it was good that Rwandans had that understanding of sacred objects. Therefore, the above reasons why Western missionaries were not in agreement with Rwandans's understanding of *Imana* show it was a false interpretation based on human error, and for Bigirumwami all humans commit mistakes. He further indicates that even if the first missionaries made errors, it is time to stop going astray and misleading Rwandans.[81] Muzungu points out how Bigirumwami used his position to help restore the use of *Imana* in place of *Mungu* as imposed by Roman Catholic missionaries:

> Mgr Bigirumwami a eu une intervention heureuse dans une Commission Liturgique Nationale qu'il présidait à Gihindamuyaga. Cette commission était chargé de trouver un vocabulaire Liturgique conforme aux recommandations du Concile Vatican II. Comme j'étais membre de cette commission, j'ai proposé qu'on revienne au nom traditionnel d'Imana dans la liturgie chrétienne, et que celui de *Mungu* soit poliment expédié à ses origines. Malgré l'opposition de quelques membres de cette commission dont Alexis KAGAME, Mgr BIGIRUMWAMI a utilisé son poids pour imposer définitivement la réhabilitation du nom Imana dans la liturgie chrétienne. Et ce fut ainsi pour de bon.[82]

> [Bishop Bigirumwami had a happy intervention in a National Liturgical Commission that he presided for at Gihindamuyaga. This commission was charged with finding a liturgical vocabulary in accordance with the recommendations of the Second Vatican Council. As a member of this commission, I proposed that we return to the traditional name of *Imana* in the Christian liturgy, and that of *Mungu* be politely sent to its origins. Despite the opposition of some members of this commission,

---

80. Bigirumwami, *Umuntu*, 107.

81. Bigirumwami, *Umuntu*, 107.

82. Muzungu, «Centenaire du Clerge Rwandais,» 47.

including Alexis KAGAME, Bishop BIGIRUMWAMI
used his weight to impose definitively the rehabilitation
of the name *Imana* in the Christian liturgy. And that
was so for good.]

Priest Alexis Kagame was and still is considered Rwanda's
leading scholar, and he favored the use of *Mungu* instead of *Imana*.
But, due to the fact that Bigirumwami had the higher position as
bishop and chairperson of the commission, he was willing to support the proposition of priest Muzungu and return to the use of
Imana as in pre-missionary times.

Rwandan Primal Religion According to Bigirumwami

Describing Rwandan primal religion, Bigirumwami indicates that:

> Idini y'Abanyarwanda ili mu idini ya ADAMU navuze
> mu No 60. Idini y'Abanyarwanda nyishyize hagati y'iya
> AYABAYAHUNDI n'IVANJILI ya Yezu Kristo, kuko ifite
> imico n'imvugo n'ingiro bihuje na Bibliya Ntagatifu. Ni
> byiza kubimenya.[83]

> [Rwandan religion is in ADAM'S religion as I discussed
> in no. 60. (It is in no. 59 that Bigirumwami discusses
> Adam's religion, not in no. 60 as he points it out here. For
> Bigirumwami, Adam's religion is natural religion written
> in the heads and hearts of people (natural revelation).) I
> put Rwandan religion between the JEWISH one and the
> GOSPEL of Jesus Christ, because in pre-colonial Rwandan religion words and deeds are in accord with the Holy
> Bible. It is good to know it.]

For Bigirumwami, Rwandan primal religion is in accord with
the Old Testament. Bigirumwami pointed out that there are images or shadows of the New Testament in the Old Testament and in
primal religion.[84] Concerning the Old Testament, he pointed out
that the first Adam was a fully human being created from the soil

83. Bigirumwami, *Umuntu*, 99.
84. Bigirumwami, *Umuntu*, 91.

and after his death he returned to the soil, but the second Adam (Jesus) was from heaven and went back to heaven. Isaac's sacrifice was an image of Jesus Christ. Joseph, who was sold by his brothers and taken away in Egypt, was a portrayal of how Jesus Christ would be denied and betrayed by his own people. Moses delivering Israelites from Egyptian slavery was the image of Jesus Christ, who is ready to save all those who believe in him from slavery of sin. The lamb of Passover in Old Testament is a symbol of Jesus Christ, just as the crossing of the Jordan River from Egypt to Canaan is a symbol of Baptism.[85] Bigirumwami further indicates that in "pagan" religions also there are images or shadows of the New Testament. Concerning Rwanda, he pointed out that the offering to ancestors through *Kuragura inka, intama*, meaning divination using cows and sheep, which are killed and offered to ancestors, are sacrifices. *Guterura umwana*, meaning holding a child after eight days of birth to prevent those who want to empoison the child from reaching him/her, as well as eating meat together during *Kubandwa*, were, for Bigirumwami, all practices that are found in Old Testament as the symbols of Jesus Christ.[86] Therefore, for him there were shadows of Christ in the Old Testament and in Rwandan primal religion. This explains why Bigirumwami kept repeating that "Jesus Christ did not come to abolish but to accomplish."[87] He clarifies this as follows:

> Ivanjili ya Yezu ntiyaje gukura ibyari biliho bikomeye, ntiyaje gusenya ibyaliho, ntiyaje gusambura ibyali bisakaye. Invanjili ya Yezu, lero Yezu ubwe, yaje gukomeza ibyiza byose byaliho, yaje kwuzuza ibyiza byali bituzuye, yaje gusoza ibyali byaranze kugira umusozo, yaje guhugura no gusobanura ibyali bisobetse mu bwenge bw'abantu no mu mitima y'abantu.[88]

> [The gospel of Jesus did not come to remove what was there, the gospel did not come to destroy what was

85. Bigirumwami, *Umuntu*, 91–92.
86. Bigirumwami, *Umuntu*, 92.
87. Bigirumwami, *Imana y 'abantu*, 71.
88. Bigirumwami, *Imana y 'abantu*, 71.

there, and the gospel did not come to remove the roof
of what was covered. The gospel of Jesus, meaning Jesus
himself, came to strengthen all the good that existed;
he came to complete good things that were incomplete,
he came to accomplish things that were without end,
he came to train and explain what was hidden in the
intellect and hearts of people.]

Defining the gospel, Kwame Bediako indicates that "the Gospel is the person of Jesus Christ of Nazareth, his ministry, his death,
his, resurrection and its aftermath, as given us in the Scriptures."[89]
For Bigirumwami also the gospel is Jesus Christ himself. Therefore,
Jesus Christ was to be an example for all engaged in the ministry of
carrying on his mission on earth. For Bigirumwami people gained
some images of Jesus Christ from OT and their primal religions,
so there was no need to consider their traditions as evil, but rather
they should be studied and used as a point of contact in spreading
the gospel. For him, it was not only Rwandans who were not able
to understand God well, but all human beings had some hidden
knowledge of Christ in their intellect and hearts that Christ came
to reveal to them. It was important to engage with people by considering the fact that they do have an idea of God, and to bring
them to Christ for full understanding.

For Bigirumwami, Rwandan religion applied not only in
Rwanda, for the four million Rwandans at the time, but also to the
more than ten million people from Burundi, Tanzania, DR-Congo,
and Uganda who practiced the same religion.[90] He further indicated that even though the Christians are the majority in Europe,
primal practices are still being carried out. As example, Bigirumwami mentioned the book of Papus Docteur Encause (1865–1916),
Comment on Lit dans la Main[91] *(How to Read in the Palms)*, used in

89. Bediako, "Gospel and Culture," 1–17(8).

90. Bigirumwami, *Umuntu*, 99.

91. Bigirumwami indicates that there is "chiromancie" [chiromancy] in
Papus's book. He further indicates that in the book there is a horoscope that
indicates how are and will be people who were born on given day in a given
month. *Umuntu*, 66. Chiromancy is devination perfomed by examining the
lines in the palms.

divination by people who want to know what will happen to them. One might argue that those who are doing so are not Christians. He further indicates what he observed in Rome at Saint Peter's Cathedral. On the iron statue of Peter the toes had all worn away as a result of the respect and love that Christians from all over the world have for Peter, which they have shown by touching and kissing them. He indicated that he also touched and kissed his feet. He further pointed out that he observed on Mount Mons near Hotel de Ville in Belgium that there was a gorilla statue, which many people kept touching to ensure a successful day and to overcome all their problems. He concluded, *"ruri hose,"* meaning "it is everywhere."[92] For Bigirumwami the primal understanding is evident not only among Africans but in all humanity, Westerners included.

Throughout the two books *Umuntu* and *Imana Y'Abantu–Abantu mu Mana* and his article "Rites, Proverbes et Fables au Rwanda," Bigirumwami kept pointing out that he was not propagating or defending paganism by indicating that Rwandan primal religion was not entirely evil.[93] While it was difficult to write critically about Bigirumwami during his lifetime, he was aware that there were other clergy who were unhappy with his publications on Rwanda primal religion. Bigirumwami first pointed out the critics and defended himself:

> Je comprends ceux qui critiquent et je support volontiers tous les reproches et toutes les attaques ecclésiastiques et civiles : 'ubuze icyo atuka inka agira ngo dore icyo gicebe cyayo'- une vache laitière ne regrettera jamais d'être une bonne laitière . . . ceux qui considèrent, après mes publications, comme un pauvre Evêque, innovateur et néo-payen, ou comme propagateur des récits et expression, indécents qui scandalisent les âmes innocents, qu'ils sachent: . . . je veux être ce prêtre et cet Evêque qui désire ardemment voir les traditions Africaines connues dans leurs valeurs et reconnues pour leur valeurs. Je veux voir et faire voir d'un bon œil les valeurs morales et religieuses africaines prise en considération et exploitées ; car

92. Bigirumwami, *Umuntu*, 66.

93. Bigirumwami, «Rites, Proverbes et Fables,» 12.

l'africain devenu chrétien n'a pas a se renier lui-même, mais a reprendre les ancien valeurs de la tradition "en esprit et en vérité."[94]

[I understand those who criticize and willingly accept all reproaches and all ecclesiastical and civil attacks: *"ubuze icyo atuka inka agira ngo dore icyo gicebe cyayo"*—a dairy cow will never regret being a good dairy . . . those who consider me, as a result of my publications, as a poor bishop, innovator, and neopagan, or as propagator of the indecent narratives and expressions that scandalize the innocent souls, let them know: . . . I want to be this priest and this bishop who longs to see the African traditions known in their values and recognized for their values. I want to see people take a good look at African moral and religious values so they may be taken into consideration and exploited; because the African who has become a Christian does not have to deny himself, but to revisit the old values of the tradition "in spirit and in truth."]

Though criticized by some of his colleagues in the ministry, for Bigirumwami there was no reason to insist that Africans experience an identity crisis in the name of Christianizing them. Therefore, he fought for African traditions and moral and religious values to be appreciated so that Africans who convert to Christianity need not to renounce what they are. After his presentation during the Recyclage Sacerdotal at Nyundo in 1969, there was an exchange with the participants, who came to this observation:

Les coutumes payenne ne sont pas encore abandonées. On le constate au confessionnal. Par exemple au moment du mariage, rares sont ceux qui ne doublent pas le sacrement de mariage de coutumes traditionnelles pratiquées chez eux, sauf quelques chrétiens bien convaincus.[95]

[Pagan customs are not yet abandoned. It can be seen in the confessional. For example, at the time of marriage, few are those who do not double the sacrament

94. Bigirumwami, «Rites, Proverbes et Fables,» 12.
95. Bigirumwami, «Rites, Proverbes et Fables,» 13.

of marriage with traditional customs practiced at home.
The exception is a few convinced Christians.]

Though many Rwandans were converting to Christianity, it
could still be observed that they were still holding on to their traditional customs. This corroborates Gillian Bediako's observation
that the primal is the "fundamental substratum to all subsequent
religious experience, continuing to varying degree in all later religious traditions."[96] The primal cannot be suppressed or eradi-
cated, as it keeps changing in later religions, Christianity included.
This is why the participants further indicated that:

> D'où l'urgence d'une catéchèse adapté qui montre
> l'inanité de la plupart de ces pratiques. Il est inefficace
> de condamner purement et simplement telle ou telle
> pratique payenne sans la remplacer positivement par
> une pratique Chrétienne. On tint à excuser les premiers
> missionnaires au sujet de l'adaptation du langage : ils
> devaient présenter un message tout neuf avec des mots
> qu'ils pouvaient trouver sur place, en faisant eux-mêmes
> l'apprentissage de la langue locale. Aujourd'hui, les tra-
> ducteurs n'ont pas les mêmes excuses ! Ils devraient nous
> présenter des traductions vraiment pastorales. L'exemple
> de la traduction fort réussie du canon Romain, montre
> que de telles traductions sont possibles ![97]

> [Hence the urgency of an adapted catechesis that shows
> the futility of most of these practices. It is ineffective to
> purely and simply condemn this or that particular pagan
> practice without replacing it positively by a Christian
> practice. We are hereby excusing the first missionaries
> on the subject of adaptation of the language: they had
> to present a brand new message with words they could
> find on the spot, learning the local language themselves.
> Today, translators do not have the same excuses! They
> should present us with truly pastoral translations. The
> example of the very successful translation of the Roman
> canon shows that such translations are possible!]

96. Bediako, "Primal Religion and Christian Faith," 12.

97. Bigirumwami, «Rites, Proverbes et Fables,» 13.

For the participants at the Nyundo conference on Christianity and traditional culture, there was a need for a well-adapted catechism and good translation of the Bible in order to engage well with Rwandan primal religion. They agreed with Bigirumwami that spreading Christianity in Rwanda using foreign languages was not a good strategy. They also agreed with Bigirumwami that some traditional practices were futile, though Bigirumwami preferred the term "little knowledge." For Bigirumwami, mother tongue was very important in the spread and adaptation of the gospel of Jesus Christ in Africa, because when people are taught in their language it easily reaches their hearts. Bigirumwami was unhappy with the fact that in 1980s the mother tongue was not used in Rwandan high school, especially in teaching religion. Why did Bigirumwami want Kinyarwanda to be used in education? In discussing *idini y'Abanyarwanda*, meaning "Rwandan religion," he indicates that:

> Idini y'abanyarwanda, izwi n'abanyarwanda. Barayihererekanya mu mvugo no mu ngiro, nk'uko bahererekanya ibindi byose. Idini y'abanyarwanda ifite ishuli mu ngo z'ababyeyi no mu ngo z'abaturanyi . . . abana bakuru b'abakobwa, bigisha abana bato b'abakobwa; abana bakuru b'abahungu bakigisha abana bato b'abahungu. Abagabo na bo bakagira ishuli lyabo, abagore na bo bakagira ilyabo. Bityo, bityo . . .[98]

> [Rwandan religion is known by Rwandans. They transmit it in their words/speech and deeds as they transmit everything to one another. Rwandan religion has a school in parents' homes, and neighbors' homes . . . older girls teach the younger ones; older boys teach the younger. It is the same for men; they have their school and women also have their school . . .]

Bigirumwami's point here is that Rwanda schools should be used to transmit Christianity from one generation to the next just like pre-colonial Rwandan religion was handed down by one generation to the next. Thus Kinyarwanda language was very important because Bigirumwami was very aware of the oral tradition

---

98. Bigirumwami, *Umuntu*, 99.

nature of Rwandan society. Concerning the "schools" of Rwandan primal religion, Bigirumwami identified equivalences for each level: *Ishuli ly'ibanze* was the primary school, where parents were the main teachers; *ishuli ly'isumbuye* was the high school, which applied to large gatherings of people, for example, during weddings and all ceremonies linked to them, or during *guterura umwana*, the rite of holding a child eight days after he/she is born. *Ishuli lya kaminuza* was the university, an *Igitaramo* (event/party, gathering), in which only great men are allowed to speak due to fact that they know *kwivuga*, meaning to make speeches in *ibyivugo* (heroes'/warriors' speech). The final school was *ishuli ly'ubupfumu*, the school of divination, prophecy (*ubuhanuzi*), which was not for everyone, but only those few who claimed to have special knowledge that was impossible for others.[99]

Bigirumwami considered that to persist in teaching religion in the language of Western empires was an obstacle to the appreciation of African traditional values. African traditions were to be appreciated instead of being undermined and demonized. While he acknowledged the fact that African primal religions were of value, he also pointed out some practices that he considered without value, which were to be redeemed by the gospel of Jesus Christ.[100] Bigirumwami's observation was in the line with Vatican II and at the same time with the Lausanne Movement through the *Willowbank Report: Consultation on Gospel and Culture*, though Bigirumwami was not aware of it. It was the view of the report that "because man is God's creature, some of his culture is rich in beauty and goodness. Because he is fallen, all of it is tainted with sin and some of it is demonic."[101] Bigirumwami stressed the nature of the human being in *Umuntu*. With respect to human nature and doing evil, he considered that one should cease putting all the blame on Westerners. For him, what the Westernization and development brought by missionaries and colonizers did was to unveil the evil nature of humanity. For the case of Rwanda,

99. Bigirumwami, *Umuntu*, 99.
100. Bigirumwami, *Umuntu*, 98.
101. Lausanne Movement, *Willowbank Report*.

he gave the example of the *Rucunshu*[102] *conflict of 1897 and the 1959*[103] *revolutionary war.*[104]

It was unjust to keep considering that all evil was brought to Rwanda by Westerners through Westernization and Christianization; rather, there should be a consideration of the fact that every human being has a fallen nature, Rwandans included. In 1897 Rwanda was already in contact with the Westerners, though there were few, yet Rwandans were also responsible for the evil-doing that took place in the kingdom.

Conclusion

Bigirumwami's perceptions of Rwandan primal religion emerged during a time when everything in relation to pre-Christianity was considered "pagan." For Bigirumwami, African traditions were to be appreciated and their value recognized.

102. Rucunshu was a conflict that followed the death of King Kigeli IV Rwabugiri, in which his successor Mibambwe IV Rutarindwa was killed and replaced by Yuhi V Musinga. Muzungu indicates that "L'erreur de Rwabugili consista donc à donner à Rutarindwa comme rein-mere « adoptive » Kanjogera alors qu'il avait déjà avec elle un fils « naturel », Musinga. Cette entorse aux principes de succession est la cause indirecte du coup de force de Rucunshu par lequel Rutarindwa fut assassine et Musinga intronisé à sa place.» Muzungu, *Histoire du Rwanda Précolonial*, 283. [Rwabugili's mistake was to give Rutarindwa, Kanjogera as 'adoptive' queen mother when he already had a 'natural' son with her, Musinga. This breach of the principles of succession is the indirect cause of Rucunshu's coup by which Rutarindwa was murdered and Musinga enthroned in his place.]

103. In 1959, many Tutsi were killed and later the kingship was replaced by a republic before Rwanda was given independence in 1962. The events of 1959 were considered as revolution by some and not by others. Being one of the controversial issues in Rwandan history, Mungarurire Peter Joseph discusses "La revolution de 1959 au Rwanda." For him what happened was the mass killing of Tutsi that he considers even as genocide, therefore it was not a revolution due to fact that there was no change that was to the benefit of all Rwandans, rather only for some. Mungarurire, "Révolution de 1959 au Rwanda," 269. In the two conlficts Rwandans were the main actors, therefore Bigirumwami is highlighting the fact that before the arrival of Westerners, Rwandans had their human failings.

104. Bigirumwami, *Umuntu*, 69.

Bigirumwami pointed out both the positive and negative sides of Rwandan primal religion. Thus, for him the negative side was not a reason for demonizing Rwandan primal religion. The images of Christ in primal religion were to serve as points of contact instead of factors denying the natural revelation of God. Therefore, for the inculturation of Christianity in Rwanda, it was very important to know the legacy of Rwandan ancestors and use it as a foundation for spreading the gospel in such way as to help Africans, Rwandans in particular, retain the positive practices of their culture.

4

The Legacy and Relevance of Aloys Bigirumwami as a Theologian

Introduction

BIGIRUMWAMI, WHO WAS TAKEN to seminary school when he was ten years old, received a Western education, which made him a foreigner in the land of his ancestors. After his training and ordination as a Roman Catholic priest, he started persecuting Rwandan traditional practices on the grounds that they were evil. Yet, through careful study, he ceased condemning the so-called evil practices when his perception of them changed and he started to appreciate the fact that Rwandan primal religion was not entirely evil; rather, it was very similar to Jewish and Old Testament religion. Bigirumwami's conversion concerning Rwandan primal religion started when he was at Muramba serving as head parish priest and continued after he was appointed as the bishop of the Nyundo diocese. As he indicates, it was the outcomes of Vatican II (1959), the views of Pope Paul VI, and some missiologists's writings that played a remarkable role in his new perceptions concerning African primal religions, especially Rwandan primal religion. As Bigirumwami grew older and assumed leadership positions, his awareness of the importance of the mother tongue for the understanding of the gospel of Jesus Christ was also growing. He therefore promoted the reading and writing of Kinyarwanda through his publications, such as his books and the journals *Hobe*, for young people, and *Bene Rugo*, for families. The journal *Cum Paraclito*, for intellectuals, used French. Concerning *Cum Paraclito*, Muzungu indicates that "Enlightened by the Holy Spirit, Bishop Bigirumwami intended to discuss, reflect and start some new pastoral and catechetical innovations. Until that time, a review of this type was unknown in Rwanda."[1] This indicates how deeply Bigirimwami was concerned for the inculturation of the gospel in the Rwandan context, reaching out to different groups of people in different ways.

In connection to the research questions, the second chapter, particularly the part that deals with the spread of Christianity in Rwanda, addressed the first question. The Western missionaries, both Roman Catholic and Protestant, had negative views of Rwandan primal religion. This made them demonize it and as a result made the first Rwandan Christians renounce their traditions. Bigirumwami is a good example of how the first converts to Christianity in Rwanda faced an identity crisis as they became like foreigners in their own country. The third and fourth chapters addressed the second question. Seeing Kinyarwanda as the vehicle to the primal worldview of Rwandans made it possible for Bigirumwami to start having positive view towards Rwandan primal religion. Bigirumwami went to the level of apologizing for having opposed Christianity to Rwandan primal religion. He noticed that trying to eradicate Rwandan primal religion was not good, as it weakened the Christian faith in Rwanda, which, he was sad to realize, was still not rooted after many years of presence in the country. He understood, as Kwame Bediako later put it, that "our primal cultural heritage is in fact the very place where Christ desires to meet us in order to transform us into his own image."[2] Bigirumwami's repentance indicates that he came to this observation and thus repented of trying to be Christian by trying to transform Rwandan Christians through the imposition of a Western model of Christianity. He therefore called upon those involved in the mission of spreading the gospel in Rwanda to take note of the

1. Muzungu, "Bishop Aloys Bigirumwami," 64.
2. Bediako, "Why Has the Summer Ended," 7.

importance of Kinyarwanda and Rwandan primal religion for the inculturation of Christianity in Rwanda.

Legacy and Relevance of Bigirumwami as Theologian

In this book, I have focused on Bigirumwami's advocacy for mother tongue use and his perceptions on Rwandan primal religion. I have pointed out his struggle for the inculturation of Christianity in Rwanda, which makes him one of the first theologians and servants of God who started this process of inculturation of the gospel in Rwanda. Discussing Bigirumwami, his colleagues in the priesthood noted, "Mgr A. Bigirumwami passera dans l'histoire de l'Eglise au Rwanda comme un apôtre infatigable de l'inculturation du message chrétien"[3] [Bishop Bigirumwami will go down in the history of the church in Rwanda as an indefatigable apostle of the inculturation of the Christian message]. It is worth pointing out that though Bigirumwami was among the first to start the process of inculturating the gospel in Rwanda, Bernardin Muzungu stood on Bigirumwami's and Alexis Kagame's shoulders and wrote many articles in the area of inculturation. Bigirumwami laid the foundation through his collections on Rwandan culture and his books and articles. In his article "Le Centenaire du Clergé Rwandais" ["The Centenary of the Rwandan Clergy"], Muzungu classified Roman Catholic clergy according to four areas of their intellectual activity: the fields of health, music, literature and history, and theology and inculturation. In the field of health, he mentions three examples: Télesphore Kayinamura, Thomas Bazarusanga, and Jean Marie Durand; in the field of music, Michel Seyoboka for drum music, Alfred Sebakiga and Eustache Byusa for religious singing. In the field of history and literature Alexis Kagame was mentioned, and in the field of theology of inculturation Bishop Aloys Bigirumwami.[4] Muzungu also recognized Bigirumwami as

3. Editions du Secrétariat général de la CEPR, *Hommage a Mgr Aloys Bigirumwami*, 99.

4. Muzungu, «Centenaire du Clerge Rwandais,» 4.

a leading theologian of inculturation in Rwanda. Therefore, it is possible to say that in Rwandan history Bigirumwami has a truly significant place, not only as the first Rwandan Roman Catholic bishop, but as one of the outstanding theologians who promoted African and Rwandan culture.

Jesus Came to Accomplish, Not to Abolish

Scholars such as Andrew Walls, Kwame Bediako, Gillian Mary Bediako, and Philip Laryea have argued for the fact that the primal religions are fertile soil, a solid foundation for Christian faith, as societies with primal religions are open to new religions, Christianity included. They all have indicated that there are points of contact in those primal religions that may be used in reaching people with the gospel of Jesus Christ. Bigirumwami also came to understand this, as indicated in his view that Rwandans were not people without the knowledge of God and that the first Western missionaries who arrived in Rwanda were wrong in considering Rwandans as superstitious people without religious knowledge. For him, Rwandan primal religion had similarities with Adam's religion and the Israelite religion in the Old Testament. Indeed, there were images of Jesus in Rwandan primal religion as in the Old Testament. For Bigirumwami, therefore, it was important to spread Christianity in Rwanda in a way that does not abolish the good elements, but rather strengthens them and also redeems those that were not in accord with the gospel of Jesus Christ. What was considered "paganism" was seen as having value that was to be appreciated by Africans/Rwandans and also non-Africans. In summary, Bigirumwami saw the image of Jesus Christ in Rwandan primal religion. It was his conviction that Christianity has to be adapted in the Rwandan context so that Rwandans could cease being nominal Christians and cease renouncing their country's good culture in the name of Christianity. This understanding is very important for helping Rwandans understand that Christianity is not to be seen as a Western religion but rather that it belongs to them and they may contribute to it.

In his position as leader and theologian Bigirumwami, will be remembered as the one who made it possible for the name for God *Imana* to be used in Roman Catholic masses and the translation of *Bibiliya Ntagatifu*, meaning the Holy Bible, and as the first Christian leader to organize a conference on "Christianity and Traditional Culture" in Rwanda, the Recyclage Sacerdotal sur Culture Traditionnelle et Christianisme (Nyundo, 1969) in which clergy and lay collaborators in the apostolate participated. The conference recommendations contributed to a successful Bible translation on the side of Roman Catholic Church, due to the fact that it took seriously Rwandan cultural terminology.

Bigirumwami: A Prophet Whose Voice Was Not Heard by Rwandans

In 1994, Rwanda, a small country, as yet not known worldwide by many people, became notorious as a result of the inhumanity that was manifested by those who planned and carried out the genocide perpetrated against the Tutsi in Rwanda. Rwanda had been praised as a Christian nation[5] in the early 1990s. Yet in his confession concerning the fact that he realized that opposing Christianity to Rwandan primal religion was wrong, Bigirumwami struck a sad note: "I regret to notice that Christianity is not rooted in Rwanda, despite many years of presence."[6] He called upon all people involved in the ministry of spreading the gospel of Jesus Christ to take note, but his voice was not heard at the time. His observation that many Rwandans were nominal Christians due to the failure to inculculate the gospel was the reason why he put so much effort into inculturation, but few Rwandan clergy were able to follow his approach. Even Bernardin Muzungu, who followed his path, was not heard, for two main reasons: he did not hold a high position like Bigirumwami, and he had to flee the country

---

5. Rutayisire, *Catholisme Rwandaise*, 257.
6. Bigirumwami, *Umuntu*, 99.

to save his life. He returned to Rwanda after the 1994 genocide against the Tutsi was over.

Bigirumwami foresaw the danger ahead. In 1959 he was one of leaders who played a role in calling for peace among Rwandans, when many Tutsi were being killed or sent out of the country. For Muzungu, "Bigirumwami did everything possible in his power to stop the genocide in 1959. Therefore in 1994, there were no strong religious leaders like him who could raise their voices and use their position to stop the genocide."[7] Writing about the effect of failing to hear Bigirumwami, Muzungu indicates that "If we had understood the words of our venerable bishop, that 'all men without exception, are created in the image of God' (*abantu bose, baremwemo umutima n'ubwenge biva ku Mana*), we would not have listened to the aberrations that we know: 'they (Tutsi) are evil by nature . . . they are snakes . . .'"[8] Bigirumwami made it clear that all human beings have both good and evil in them, but during the 1994 genocide against Tutsi some people were considered entirely evil. Muzungu is right that ignoring or not listening to the voice of Bigirumwami is one of the factors that led to the horror that Rwandans went through when the genocide perpetrated against Tutsi was carried out in 1994.

Advocate of Mother Tongue Use

Bigirumwami is among the few Rwandans who came to the realization that "you need to speak the language of the people if you want to reach their hearts." For Bigirumwami Kinyarwanda was a vehicle to the *Munyarwanda*; it was not possible to think, talk, like, and engage with the *Munyarwanda* without the language Kinyarwanda. A Rwandan community designs and furnishes its own world. That is, a community decides what is good, what is bad, what is important, what is unimportant, and who should behave in certain ways. The rain falling from the sky, the immersion

7. Muzungu, conversation, July 9, 2018, Kigali.

8. Muzungu, "Bishop Aloys Bigirumwami," 73.

of a person in water, words spoken by an old person; these have no meaning apart from the value given to them by the community and its individual members. Thus, a Rwandan community creates its own interpretation of life, its own view of the world. Therefore, for Bigirumwami, even in school, religion should be taught in Kinyarwanda so that Rwandan children may appreciate well the value of their Rwandan traditions. As we pointed it out in the general introduction, all Rwandans use one language, Kinyarwanda. Having one language is helpful not only for the unity of the country but for the mission of making disciples of Christ in Rwanda. Thus, we need to value what Bigirumwami is pointing out to us in our generation, where, due to globalization, English tends to dominate at the expense of Kinyarwanda, especially among the youth. In his article "Tasks of a Theologian in Africa Today," Jimi Zacka indicates that:

> It is urgent that Africa has to re-build its cultural, economical, social, and political ruins, from the destroyed infrastructures to broken societies. This task calls for a new form of theological discourse that must be developed by African theologians. Because, today, we notice that African theology, like other theologies, predominantly remains an intellectual exercise. Indeed it seems to have become 'a theology of theologians, by theologians, for theologians', instead of becoming 'a theology of the people, by the people, for the people'. Thus, we think that the task of the African theologian today is to initiate a new perspective that can transform the social life, and to initiate a discipleship of equals and the eradication of mass poverty. That can help Christians to build an open society, which meets the needs of people, and restores their human dignity. It could be called a theology of responsibility.[9]

By "theologians," Zacka is referring to those involved in academia or trained theologians, but it is noteworthy to point out the fact that everyone can theologize, especially when the mother tongue is given much attention. From the above quotation, we

9. Zacka, "Tasks of a Theologian."

notice that one of the major tasks of African theologians is to move from "a theology of theologians . . . for theologians" to "a theology of the people . . . for the people." It is impossible for theology to be for people when their mother tongue is neglected. Therefore, it is time for African theologians to theologize in their mother tongue, so that theology will be for people in Africa, Rwanda particularly. For Zacka, a theology of responsibility is needed; I will add that one of the responsibilities is to promote the use of the mother tongue in the academic sector. Theses, papers, and seminars using the mother tongue are needed from theologians so that they cease being Africans speaking in Western languages in the name of African theology. Bigirumwami helps us see that there is no African theology without giving our mother tongue the first place. If we keep our mother tongue in second or third place, Christianity will continue to be a foreign religion to Africans, thus it will not reach their hearts in order to transform their sociocultural, political, and economic sectors.

Scholarship and Mission

For Andrew Walls, "it is the essence of the Gospel that God accepts us as we are, on the grounds of Christ's work alone, not on the grounds of what we have become or are trying to become."[10] In the Rwandan case, people were not accepted as they were by missionaries. The only way to become a Christian was to separate from the past; therefore force was used. God doesn't need to use force or to force us to renounce who we are before accepting us.

This study is therefore important as it help us to appreciate the elements of pre-colonial Rwandan primal religion collected and published by Bigirumwami, which may serve as areas of further research for suitable inculturation. By examining Bigirumwami's advocacy of mother tongue use and his perceptions of Rwandan primal religion, we hope to enhance the Christian mission in Africa and specifically in Rwanda. The 1994 genocide against the

10 Walls, *Missionary Movement in Christian History*, 7.

Tutsi was the major factor indicating that Rwandans were not well evangelized. This resounds in Bishop Aloys Bigirumwami's confession and warning to church leaders to take note. However, he remained the rare church leader in Rwanda who sought to raise awareness until the genocide against the Tutsi occurred. Therefore, this study has drawn new insights from Bigirumwami's works that may help the Rwandan church, which at present still lacks connection with the "fundamental substratum" of indigenous religion and culture for carrying out the task of mission. I hope that this work will be useful to the church in Rwanda, as there is a need to revisit its views toward the Rwandan primal religions, and the Rwandan past in general, so that we may be "able to relate to our past" and deepen the Christian faith in Rwanda.

In discussing the universal relevance of the gospel, Bediako indicates that "it is this task of demonstrating the universal relevance of the gospel that makes translation and other theological activities in the mother tongue of such vital importance for overcoming the assumption that the Christian faith is the religion of the West."[11] This study being in the area of mother tongue and primal riligion has sought to point out to Rwandans that Christianity as a religion was spread in Rwanda by Western missionaries, but Jesus Christ as God and Son of God was already in Rwanda before their arrival. So, it is important to consider Christianity as a universal religion and to know that all good things can't only stem from Western countries.[12]

About the importance of mother tongue use for the inculturation of Christian faith, Bediako indicates that the Bible in

11. Bediako, "Christian Faith and African Culture," 45.

12. This is important because there are many facts of daily life that indicate that Rwandans are more Westernized, to the extent of considering everything from the West as good. For example, Rwandan names like Kubwimana, Ndizeye, and Bigirumwami are till today called pagan names, whereas Western names like Peter, Jean, Joel, Aloys, are called Christian names. A local cow is called *Inyarwanda* and considered inferior due to their low productivity. The prized cows are called *inzungu*, meaning "white people's cows," and considered as good ones. A tradition hen is called *inshenzi, inyarwanda* and the prized ones *inzungu* even if the selection is done in Rwanda by Rwandans. I can point out many other examples to illustrate this.

the mother tongue brought people back to their own roots, past, present, and future.[13] He continues and shows that "Scripture is not only a text that modern Christians may appropriate through the requisite skills and techniques of exegesis and hermeneutics; Scripture is also a context in which modern Christians can share as illuminating of their own human experience."[14] The context in which people live is important and is to be taken into consideration, not only in Bible translation and interpretation but in all activities of carrying on the Great Commission given to us by Jesus Christ in Matthew 28:18–20. Globalization is making English as a "new Latin" in church life, but for Bediako:

> If there is any merit in the concept of the Scriptures as also context, that persons of varied cultural backgrounds can enter and participate in, bringing their own cultural worlds of meaning with them, then it can be said that the exegesis of biblical texts may not be taken as completed when one established meanings in Hebrew, Aramaic and Greek. Instead, the process needs to continue into all possible languages in which biblical faith is received, mediated and expressed.[15]

According to Bediako, the translation process needs to continue, since by promoting one particular language only the church will deprive itself of the opportunity for new theological insights.[16] In this study I have stressed the fact that the mother tongue is the vehicle to the primal imagination of people; therefore, as Bediako indicates that translation needs to continue, inculturation of the gospel also needs to continue. Bigirumwami, in his time, among his generation, worked hard for gospel inculturation by advocating for mother tongue use and the appreciation of African, particularly Rwanda, traditions and values.

In concluding his article "The Bible and African Cultural Identity in a Globalised World," Roy Musasiwa indicates that "while the

13. Bediako, "Biblical Exegesis," 17.
14. Bediako, "Biblical Exegesis," 18.
15. Bediako, "Biblical Exegesis," 18.
16. Bediako, "Biblical Exegesis," 19.

forces of globalisation are a threat to African cultural identity, the Bible should be legitimately used in defense of such identity."[17] He further points out that "this can only happen, however, when the Bible is interpreted in a way that makes it contextually relevant to our context. Otherwise, the Bible would either remain irrelevant to our quest for identity, or at worst be abused by dominant forces of globalisations in the destruction of such identity."[18] Therefore, it is our responsibility during our time, our generation, to take up the task and continue this process of contextualising the gospel, which will end in heaven when "great multitude that no one could count, from every nation, tribe, people and language, [stands] before the throne and the Lamb wearing white robes and holding palm branches in their hands" (Rev 7:9). Let us do our task of discipling the nations so that our nations, our languages, our people will be among those who will stand before the throne and the Lamb.

17. Musaswa, "Bible and African Cultural Identiy," 19.
18. Musaswa, "Bible and African Cultural Identiy," 19.

Bibliography

Akimana, Gabriel. "Translation Issues in an Interconfessional Bible Version: An Evaluation of *Bibiriya Ijambo ry 'Imana* Through a Hebrew–Kinyarwanda Analysis of Selected Passages." PhD diss., Akrofi-Christaller Institute of Theology, Culture and Mission, Akropong–Akuapem, 2016.

Amidu, Assibi A. "Kiswahili: People, Language, Literature and Lingua Franca." *Nordic Journal of African Studies* 4/1 (1995) 104–23. http://www.njas. helsinki.fi.

Bainton, Roland H. *Christendom: A Short History of Christianity and Its Impact on Western Civilization.* New York: Harper & Row, 1966.

Becker, Michael K. "Episcopal Unrest: Gallicanism in the 1625 Assembly of the Clergy." *Church History* 43/1 (March 1974) 65–77.

Bede, Saint. *A History of the English Church and People.* Translated by Leo Sherley-Price, revised by R. E. Latham. London: Penguin Classics, 1955.

Bediako, Gillian M. "Biblical Exegesis in the African Context: The Factor and Impact of the Translated Scripture. *JACT* 6/1 (June 2003) 15–23.

———. "Christian Faith and African Culture: An Exposition of the Epistle to Hebrews." *JACT* 13/1 (June 2010) 45–57.

———. *Christianity in Africa: The Renewal of a Non-Western Religion.* Akropong-Akuapem/Ghana: Regnum Africa, 2014.

———. "Primal Religion and Christian Faith: Antagonists or Soul-Mates?" *JACT* 3/1 (June 2000) 12–16.

———. *Primal Religion and the Bible: William Robertson Smith and His Heritage.* Sheffield: Sheffield Academic, 1997.

———. "The Relationship between Primal Religion and Biblical Religion in the Works of William Robertson Smith." PhD diss., University of Aberdeen, 1995.

———. *Theology and Identity: The Impact of Culture upon Christian Thought in the Second Century and in Modern Africa.* Oxford: Regnum, 1999.

———. "Why Has the Summer Ended and We Are Not Served? Encountering the Real Challenge of Christian Engagement in a Primal Context." *JACT* 11/2 (December 2008) 5–8.

Bediako, Gillian M., B. Y. Quarshie, and A. Gyadu Kwabena, eds. *Seeing New Facets of the Diamond: Christianity as a Universal Faith.* Oxford/Akropong: Regnum/Regnum Africa, 2014.

Bediako, Kwame. "Gospel and Culture: Some insights for Our Time from the Experience of the Early Church." *JACT* 2/2 (December 1999) 1–17.

Bigirumwami, Aloys. "A mes Frères dans le Sacerdoce." Nyundo, October 7, 1967.

———. *Imana y'Abantu, Abantu b'Imana, Imana mu Bantu, Abantu mu Mana.* Nyundo: 1976.

———. *Imihango Idakwiye Hommage reconnaissance aux Vénérés vicaires Apostoliques d'heureuse Mémoire.* Nyundo, 1964.

———. *Imihango yo mu Rwanda, Kuragura Guterekers, Kubandwa, Nyabingi, igitabo cya kabiri.* Nyundo, 1968.

———. *Imihango, n'Imigenzo n'Imiziririzo mu Rwanda.* Nyundo, 1984. 4th ed., reprinted 2014.

———. "Rites, Proverbes, et Fables au Rwanda." In *Culture traditionnelle et Christianisme: Actes du Recyclage sacerdotal de Nyundo,* 3–12. Nyundo, 1969.

———. *Umuntu: Balibwira-Barabwirwa-Batereliyo ni Jyejyewe-Jyejyenyine.* Nyundo, 1983.

Birikunzira, Jérôme. "L'Église Adventiste du 7e Jour au Rwanda." In *Histoire du Christianisme au Rwanda: Des Origines à nos Jours,* edited by Tharcisse Gatwa and Laurent Rutinduka, 97–116. Yaoundé: Editions CLE, 2014.

Bushayija, Antoni B. *Musenyeri Aloyizi Bigirumwami.* Toulouse: Izuba éditions, 2014.

Byanafashe, Déogratias. "La Methodologie de l'Histoire face a l'historiographie rwandaise." In *Les défis de l'Historiographie rwandaise,* 15–28. Butare/Rwanda, Editions de L'Université Nationale du Rwanda, 2004.

———. Byanafashe, Déogratias "Presentation." In Déogratias Byanafashe, *Les défis de l'Historiographie rwandaise,* 7–28. Butare/Rwanda: Editions de L'Université Nationale du Rwanda, 2004.

Byanafashe, Déogratias, et al., eds. "The Teaching of History of Rwanda, A Participatory Approach a Resource Book for Teachers for Secondary Schools in Rwanda." Regents of the University of California, 2006. See https://www.law.berkeley.edu.

Byanafashe, Déogratias, and Paul Rutayisire, eds. *History of Rwanda: From the Beginning to the End of the Twentieth Century History of Rwanda.* Kigali: National Unity and Reconciliation Commission, 2016. See http://www.nurc.gov.rw.

Commission Nationale de Recensement. *3ème Recensement générale de la population et de l'habitat du Rwanda 15 Aout 2002 Etat et structure de la population.* Kigali : Février 2005.

Corten, André. "Rwanda: Du réveil est-africain au pentecôtisme." *Canadian Journal of African Studies / Revue Canadienne des Études Africaines* 37/1 (2003) 28–47.

Cragg, Kenneth. *Christianity in World Perspective.* London: Lutterworth, 1968.

Cusack, M. Carole. *The Rise of Christianity in Northern Europe, 300–1000.* London: Cassell, 1998.

Daly, William M. "Clovis: How Barbaric, How Pagan?" *Speculum* 9/3 (July 1994) 619–64.

Delforge, Jacques, ed. *Le Rwanda Tel Qu'ils L'ont Vu: Un siècle de regards européens 1862–1962.* Paris: L'Harmattan, 2008.

Editions du Secrétariat général de la CEPR. *Hommage a Mgr Aloys Bigirumwami première Evêque rwandais, témoignages recueillis a l'occasion du Jubile de 50 ans de l'Institution de la Hiérarchie ecclésiastique au Rwanda (1959–2009).* Kigali : Editions du Secrétariat général de la CEPR, 2009.

Gasore, Louis. *Umukristu mu ba mbere bo mu Rwanda: Yozefu Rukamba.* Nyundo, 1968.

Gatwa, Tharcisse. *The Churches and Ethnic Ideology in the Rwandan Crises 1900–1994.* London: Regnum, in association with Paternoster, 2005.

———. " L'Église Presbytérienne au Rwanda." In *Histoire du Christianisme au Rwanda: Des Origines à nos Jours*, edited by Tharcisse Gatwa and Laurent Rutinduka, 63–96. Yaoundé: Editions CLE, 2014.

Giles, Kevin. *What On Earth Is the Church?: A Biblical and Theological Enquiry.* London: SPCK, 1995.

Gregory of Tours. *The History of the Franks.* London: Penguin, 1974.

Habarurema, Viateur. "L'Église Pentecôte au Rwanda (ADEPR)." In *Histoire du Christianisme au Rwanda: Des Origines à nos Jours*, edited by Tharcisse Gatwa and Laurent Rutinduka, 177–210. Yaoundé: Editions CLE, 2014.

Henry, A. M., ed. *Vatican II: Déclaration sur les relations de l'église de Dieu avec les religions non Chrétiennes.* Paris: Edtions du Cerf, 1966.

Henry, Matthew. *Commentary on the Whole Bible.* Chicago: OM Literature, 1995.

Howell, Allison M. *The Religious Itinerary of a Ghanaian People: The Kasena and the Christian Gospel.* Accra: Africa Christian, reprinted with permission from Peter Lang, 2001.

Johnson, Frederick, et al. *A Standard Swahili-English Dictionary.* Nairobi: Oxford University Press, 1939.

Kagame, Alexis. *Inganji Kalinga.* Kabgayi, 1943.

———. *Philosophie bantu-rwandaise de l'etre.* NP: NPH, 1966.

———. *Un abgrégé de l'ethno-histoire du Rwanda.* Butare: Editions Universitaire du Rwanda, 1972.

Kalimba, Jéred. "L'Église Anglicane au Rwanda." In *Histoire du Christianisme au Rwanda: Des Origines à nos Jours*, edited by Tharcisse Gatwa and Laurent Rutinduka, 117–44. Yaoundé: Editions CLE, 2014.

Kanimba, Misago. "Peuplement et migration d'apres l'Archéologie: Cas du Rwanda." In *Les défis de l'Historiographie rwandaise*, edited by Déogratias Byanafashe, 103–24. Butare: Editions de L'Université Nationale du Rwanda, 2004.

Kanyarwanda. "Aloys Bigirumwami." http://www.kanyarwanda.net/ki/blog/2016/10/26/aloys-bigirumwami.

Kato, Byang H. *Theological Pitfalls in Africa*. Nairobi: Evangel, 1975.

Kimenyi, Alexandre. "Imana in Rwanda." http://www.kimenyi.com/imana-in-rwanda.php.

———. "Language, Names and Religious Beliefs." http://www.kimenyi.com/languagenamesreligiousbeliefs.php.

Kreider, Alan, ed. *The Origins of Christendom in the West*. Edinburgh: T. & T. Clark, 2001.

Laryea, Philip T. "Letting the Gospel Re-Shape Culture: Theological Creativity in Mother Tongue." *JACT* 4/1 (June 2001) 27–32.

Lausanne Movement. *The Willowbank Report: Consultation on Gospel and Culture*. 1978. https://www.lausanne.org/content/lop/lop-2.

Mungarurire, Josep P. "La révolution de 1959 au Rwanda." In *Les défis de l'Historiographie rwandaise*, by Déogratias Byanafashe, 269–287. Butare: Editions de L'Université Nationale du Rwanda, 2004.

Musaswa, Roy. "The Bible and African Cultural Identity in a Globalised World." *JACT* 20/2 (December 2017) 13–19.

Mutwarasibo, Ernest. "Remembering the Humanity: Accounting for Resisting Genocide in Rwanda in 1994." http://www.genociteresearchhub.org.rw.

Muzungu, Bernadin. "Bishop Aloys Bigirumwami: A Shining Star in the Political Darkness of Rwanda." *Les Cahiers Lumières et Société* 48 (May 2012) 61–85.

———. «Le Centenaire du Clerge Rwandais.» *Les Cahiers Lumières et société* 54 (January 2017) n.p.

———. *Histoire du Rwanda Précolonial*. Paris : L'Harmattan, 2003.

———. "Immana y'I Rwanda" (Dieu qui règne au Rwanda). *Cum Paraclito*, NO spécial Noel, 1965, Nyundo.

———. "La Religion Traditionnelle des Rwandais Comparée aux autres Religions." *Les Cahiers Lumière et Société* 60 (January 2011) 1–16.

Nash, Ford D. "Early British Kingdoms." http://www.earlybritishkingdoms.com.

Ngaina, Vellah T. "Bible Translation as an Inter-Religious Process: A Case Study of Mark 1:1–4 in *Biibilya Nyēē Tiliil*." *JACT* 19/2 (December 2016) 24–40.

Ngarukiyintwari, Léonidas. "Tumenye Umurage Twasigiwe n'umukurambere wacu, Musenyeri Aloys Bigirumwami." www.nyundodiocese.info.

Niyikiza, Obed. "L'Église Méthodiste au Rwanda." In *Histoire du Christianisme au Rwanda: Des Origines à nos Jours*, edited by Tharcisse Gatwa and Laurent Rutinduka, 159–75. Yaoundé: Editions CLE, 2014.

Nyundo Diocese, *Recyclage Sacerdotal sur Culture Traditionnelle et Christianisme*. Nyundo Juiellet-Aout 1969.

Pagès, G. *Un Royaume Hamite au Centre de l'Afrique.* Bruxelles: Bruxelles Falk, 1933.

Palma, Helena L. "Aspects of Multilingualism in the Democratic Republic of the Congo." 2008. https://www.semanticscholar.org/paper/Aspects-of-Multilingualism-in-the-Democratic-of-the-Palma/d5b4bc0a3f4ac60a7a4f8eb5ea151a20addc4ac9.

Pfeiffer, Charles F., and Everett F. Harrison. *The Wycliffe Bible Commentary.* Chicago: Moody, 1962.

Quarshie, B. Y. "The Bible in African Christianity: Kwame Bediako and the Reshaping of an African Heritage." *Journal of African Christian Thought* 14/2 December 2011) 1–16.

Repubulika y'u Rwanda Perezidansi ya Repubulika. *Ubumwe Bw'Abanyarwanda mbere y'Abazungu n'igihe cy'ubukoloni mu gihe cya repubulika ya mbere.* Kigali: Kanama, 1999.

Rugambage, Samuel. "L'Union des Églises Baptistes au Rwanda." In *Histoire du Christianisme au Rwanda: Des Origines à nos Jours,* edited by Tharcisse Gatwa and Laurent Rutinduka, 145–58. Yaoundé: Editions CLE, 2014.

Rutayisire, Paul. "Le catholicisme Rwandais: Un Regard Interrogateur." In *Histoire du Christianisme au Rwanda: Des Origines à nos Jours,* edited by Tharcisse Gatwa and Laurent Rutinduka, 253–354. Yaoundé: Editions CLE, 2014.

Rutinduka, Laurent. "L'Église catholique au Rwanda." In *Histoire du Christianisme au Rwanda: Des Origines à nos Jours,* edited by Tharcisse Gatwa and Laurent Rutinduka, 15–62. Yaoundé: Editions CLE, 2014.

Sanneh, Lamin. *West African Christianity: The Religious Impact.* Maryknoll, NY: Orbis, 1983.

Semujanga, Josias. "Le discours scientifique comme porteur de stéréotypes." In *Les défis de l'Historiographie rwandaise : Les faits controveresée,* by Déogratias Byanafashe, 29–54. Butare, Editions de L'Université Nationale du Rwanda, 2004.

Shimamungu, Eugène. "Biographie de Mgr Aloys Bigirumwami." http://editions-sources-du-nil.over-blog.com/article-31913892.html.

Sibo, Adrian. *Imigani y'Ikinyarwanda, n'ibisobanuro mu Cyongereza.* Kampala: Fountain, 2012.

Spijker, Gerard van't. "Is Pagan Dead? The Theological Legacy of Protestant Missionaries to Rwanda." http://gerardvantspijker.nl/fileadmin/bestanden.

Taylor, Christopher C. "Kings and Chaos in Rwanda: On the Order of Disorder." *Anthropos* 98/1 (2003) 41–58.

Taylor, John B., ed. *Primal World-Views: Christian Involvement in Dialogue with Traditional Thought Forms.* Ibadan: Daystar, 1976.

Turkson, Peter, and Frans Wijsen, eds. *Inculturation: Abide by the Otherness of Africa and the Africans.* Kampen: Kok, 1994.

Turner, Harold. "The Primal Religions of the World and Their Study." In *Australian Essays in World Religions,* edited by Victor C. Hayes. Bedford Park: Australian Association for the Study of Religions, 1977.

Walls, Andrew F. "Converts or Proselytes? The Crisis over Conversion in the Early Church." *International Bulletin of Missionary Research* 28/1 (January 2004) 2–7.

———. *The Cross-Cultural Process in Christian History.* Maryknoll, NY: Orbis, 2002; reissued by Regnum Africa, 2017.

———. *Crossing Cultural Frontiers: Studies in the History of World Christianity.* Maryknoll, NY: Orbis, 2017.

———. "The Gospel as the Prisoner and Liberator of Culture." *Southern African Journal of Mission Studies* 10/3 (November 1982) 93–105.

———. "Kwame Bediako and Christian Scholarship in Africa." *International Bulletin of Missionary Research* 32/4 (October 2008) 188–93.

———. *The Missionary Movement in Christian History: Studies in the Transmission of Faith.* Maryknoll, NY: Orbis, 1996; reissued by Regnum Africa, 2017.

Weaver, Patrick. "Henry L Gantt, 1861–1919: Debunking the Myths, a Retrospective View of His Work." *PM World Journal* 1/5 (December 2012) 1–19.

Westermann, Diedrich. "The Value of the Africa's Past." *International Review of Missions* 15/59 (July 1926) 418–37.

Williams, R. D. "The Logic of Arianism." *The Journal of Theological Studies*, n.s., 34/1 (April 1983) 56–81.

Yardeni, Myriam. «Le Christianisme De Clovis Aux XVIe et XVIIe Siècles.» *Bibliothèque de l'École des chartes* 154/1 (January–June 1996) 153–72.

Zacka, Jimi. "Tasks of a Theologian in Africa Today." December 20, 2015. https://tephila.blogspot.com/2015/12/tasks-of-theologian-in-africa-today.html.